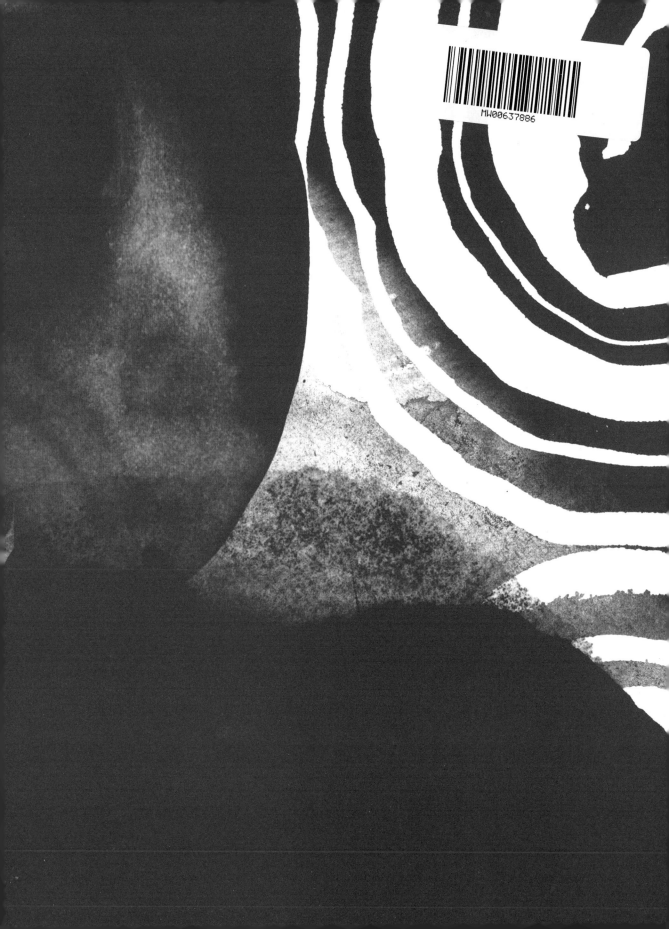

MW00637886

BAHARI

DINA MACKI

BAHARI

Recipes From an Omani
Kitchen and Beyond

CONTENTS

BAHARI
OCEAN | بحْر | BAHR

Every time I learn about a new dish, its origin and evolution, I'm always taken back to the ocean. *Bahr* (بحْر) in Arabic, *bahari* in Swahili, the sea covers 70 per cent of the globe, connecting and influencing most countries. But there is something special about Oman's relationship to the sea, and through all my travels and research for the recipes in this book, the *bahari* was the element that came up in every conversation. Whether it was the discussion of trade, merchants and history, or learning about why my family and the Omani-Zanzibari community created a life in Portsmouth in the UK, at the centre was the ocean.

From Island to Island

There is a celestial air that surrounds Oman. Maybe it's the confluence of the Persian Gulf, Arabian Sea and Indian Ocean that creates such an atmosphere, along with the myriad cultures that call this place home, weaved into such a tiny population.

Set on the southeast Arabian Peninsula, Oman meets the UAE in the north, where the Hajar Mountains overlook the Strait of Hormuz and Iran. To the west, the interior plateau extends towards vast deserts and dunes of the world's largest sand sea – an area known as Rub Al'Khali or the Empty Quarter – shared with Saudi Arabia and Yemen. This "sand sea" is the reason Oman is sometimes called an island, surrounded as it is by oceans of water and sand. The country's vast coastline stretches from the north, where the capital Muscat sits on the Gulf of Oman, to the east and south, where oceans link us to the rest of the world, most importantly to Zanzibar and, far away in the distance, Portsmouth.

I was born and raised in Portsmouth among my mother's family and their Omani-Zanzibari community – people who had migrated from the island of Zanzibar, had heritage from Oman, Iran and the Swahili coast, and were now living together on another (very cold) island, Great Britain. Each of these places are connected by the *bahari*, but there is another link that holds them together for me – the food that has been shared with me by family and friends, and which I now hope to share with you. This includes fish curries, ever-present in Muscat homes, and the street food enjoyed on the Mutrah Corniche; richly spiced, ghee-laden dishes of Oman's Interior; deliciously varied seafood found along Oman's rambling coastline; coconut- and cardamom-rich dishes of Zanzibar, where influences of the Swahili coast and Oman blend with Iranian and Indian flavours; and the recipes I grew up with in Portsmouth, as the diaspora community adapted traditional dishes to suit available ingredients and celebrate our culture. For me, *Bahari* is a way to honour my origins, as well as my mother and grandmother's home and our history.

The History of Oman

Oman's history is powerful and complex. It was a pinnacle of the Silk Road, and mustered an entire empire from its strategic geographical location; however, over the last 50 or so years, it has transitioned from a vast, far-reaching dominion to a place now known as the hidden gem of the Middle East.

The country is ancient, home to one of the earliest inhabited cities in the world – a place in the Dhofar region known as Al Wattih, which dates back 10,000 years. Throughout the Bronze and Iron Ages (3300–550 BCE), before it was called Oman, the country was known as Ancient Magan or Makkan. The word *Magan* came from Sumerian, an ancient language that predates Arabic. Magan soon became a powerful trading hub – known as the "land of copper" for its trade in the precious metal, along with gold, silver, boats and diorite (a black stone used to make statues and buildings) – and was paramount in the region, particularly for Mesopotamia. The land's population was sparse; with the arid weather conditions in the north, most people didn't settle and just came to the country for trade, which is why we now have a large Bedouin community (nomads of the desert). The country wasn't known for its food at the time, but all those travellers who came to Magan for copper brought with them recipes, cooking techniques and ingredients, all of which would ultimately help lead to the rich food culture of Oman today.

Merchants from ancient Iran, Afghanistan and the Levant all travelled to and settled in Oman, as well as the Mesopotamians, Sumerians and Persians. By the 16th century, the Portuguese had arrived from their colonies in India and settled in the north of Oman, taking over what is now the capital, Muscat, and some parts of the coast. Though Ottoman fleets repeatedly raided Muscat, the Portuguese largely retained control of the region until 1650, when they were driven out by groups under Imam rule, including the Yarubid dynasty (with ancestors from Yemen).

It was Saif bin Sultan, the Imam of the Yarubid dynasty, who had begun the mission of conquering the East African coast in around 1696, taking over Zanzibar in 1698. The decision to grow was partly a tactic to remove the Portuguese, although Saif was very focused on investing in agriculture in Oman. Since East Africa had both the perfect geographical location and climate conditions, an established network of trade between it and Oman would allow the empire to flourish.

The outbreak of civil war allowed the Persian ruler Nadir Shah to invade the country in 1737. Restoration for Oman began in 1744 when Ahmad ibn Said Al Busaidi, a governor from Sohar, the port city in the north, drove out Nadir Shah and established the Al Said dynasty (the royal family that still stands today), thus becoming the Imam of Oman, Zanzibar, Pemba and Kilwa, and continuing to expand the empire into Bahrain and parts of Iran – Bandar Abbas, Hormuz and Qeshm.

By the 19th century, Oman controlled the East African coast from Mogadishu down to Mozambique. Most countries along the coast had pledged their allegiance to Oman and were divided into smaller states. The ruling Sultan, Said ibn Sultan, had made sure to strengthen relations with each country, and when it came to Zanzibar, he invested in clove farms, as he was determined to make Zanzibar the biggest exporters of cloves in the world. As he began to spend more time on the island and see the growth in it, versus the decline in Oman, he made the decision to move his capital to Stone Town, Zanzibar, from Muscat, Oman. Omanis were encouraged to move over to Zanzibar in search of a better life, embracing the chance to build businesses and thrive. Many of them intermarried with indigenous African people (including my own family).

Others had already settled in Zanzibar, including people from Iran, Yemen, China and India, all of whom had been trading there for centuries before Oman arrived. Adding to the cloves that were the primary spice grown on the island, the Indian community brought along cinnamon, black pepper, turmeric and cardamom, while Iranians brought saffron, giving Zanzibar the name of "Spice Island". It was also a prominent place for trading enslaved people, with merchants travelling from Britain, Germany, Iran, Holland, India and elsewhere. The trade of enslaved people in Zanzibar was finally abolished in 1876.

Upon Said ibn Sultan's death in 1856, the Sultanate of Oman and Zanzibar was divided between his two sons, Majid and Thuwain, remaining under the same empire but with a separate ruler for each country. Zanzibar was a British protectorate from 1890 until 1963. After this, Zanzibar's Sultan at the time, Sultan Jamshid Al Said, took back full control of Zanzibar for just a year before the 1964 revolution by Tanganika (current-day mainland Tanzania) took place. The revolution was more of a cold-blooded war: the Black-African majority could not envision social progress while power was in Arab hands, causing them to rise up in rebellion and forcing all Omani-Zanzibaris to flee their home.

Baba Qaboos

Baba is one way of saying "father" in Arabic. In Omani households, this was how many of us informally, and lovingly, addressed our late Sultan, Qaboos. Baba Qaboos created modern-day Oman, the country we know today. On 23 July 1970,

he officially acceded to the throne, having taken the seat from his father, Said bin Taimur, who spent his remaining years in the UK. This pivotal moment for Oman led to an adoration for Qaboos that still lives on after his death. The stories you hear from people who witnessed the reigns of both Sultan Said (his father) and Sultan Qaboos will have you marvelling at how dramatically Sultan Qaboos changed their lives for the better. He created a future for the country. He introduced education for the first time, and wanted his people to have a great chance in life and to love where they were from. His father, on the other hand, had deeply feared and distrusted any form of change, including all the positive progress that was sweeping across the globe at gathering speed. This meant exercising extreme control over the people and stifling any chance at flourishing in the new world. I think having survived this suffering is partly why we have held on to our culture so strongly, as a badge of honour, and to celebrate the freedom of our families.

When Baba Qaboos died in January 2020, the sadness that swept the nation was unimaginable. His death had world leaders flying into Oman in a heartbeat to offer their condolences. It sent foreigners who had worked in or visited the country into mourning. Even our skies unleashed a torrent of tears, amid a long-running drought.

Sultan Qaboos didn't have his own offspring; his nation became his children, and he was their father. He left Omanis with a strong patriotic sense that we should help the country grow, and this is one of the reasons why Omanis are well known for studying abroad and then always returning home. So to find Omanis settled elsewhere is very rare, and it is stranger still to find a whole community like the one in Portsmouth, where I grew up.

The Omani Diaspora

In 1964, following the revolution in Zanzibar, my grandmother, Bibi, and all her friends and family witnessed the bloodshed and violence as many people tried to flee the chaos. Although it had stopped being a British protectorate a year earlier, the Omanis on the island were still supported by the British due to the strong relationship with Oman, and so all Omani families were given the opportunity to settle in Oman or join the last Sultan of Zanzibar, Jamshid, in England (Sultan Jamshid was unable to go to Oman for political reasons).

My grandfather Babu made the decision to bring his family to the UK. He was a biochemist who specialised in food canning, and had actually been sent to New York by the Zanzibari government for further studies at the time, so when the revolution broke out, he wasn't able to return to the island. Bibi had fled by boat in the night with her five children and no belongings to Mombasa, where she stayed for a year while Babu figured out their next move. Babu's family were a mix of Omani and Iranian, and he was also captain of the Zanzibar cricket team and a very big fan of the British. They arrived in the UK in April 1965 and settled in Portsmouth, along with all the rest of the Omani-Zanzibari people.

Their reasons for settling in this small coastal city came down to a man called Sheikh Salim Al Riyami, who I would later know as Babu Big, the wonderful, kindhearted pillar of our Omani-Zanzibari community. This towering, gentle man who thoroughly enjoyed his food, and whose bellowing voice would always remind me of the sound of whale song, had left Zanzibar just before the revolution. Like my grandfather, Babu Big had been sent abroad by the Zanzibari government for training, and happened to be based in Portsmouth. He developed a fond infatuation with the city, and when the Sultan of Zanzibar had to flee, Babu Big encouraged him to come to Portsmouth, as he saw vivid similarities between the two places. Indeed, both were islands and port cities, and both had a naval base and beaches (although Portsmouth lacked palm trees and sand). Essentially, both places were deeply connected to the *bahari*. Babu Big felt that the Omani-Zanzibaris would be able to come to Portsmouth and peacefully recreate something similar to what they'd once had. So Sultan Jamshid headed to the UK, and many families followed him to Portsmouth in search of community and peace. And just like that, Babu Big, our Zanzibari big friendly giant, created a safe haven for us all.

Growing Up in Portsmouth

In a bid to give me the life she and her siblings didn't have, my mother found a way to pay for me to attend a posh private school that she couldn't really afford. The only issue with this privilege was that I found myself surrounded by hundreds of children who didn't look like me nor have a home life that was anything like mine. Even the food we ate didn't smell, taste or look remotely the same.

As a teenager, those differences were bewildering, and it was one of the most embarrassing and confusing times of my life. When I was very young, I had just assumed I was exactly the same as every child I sat with in class. As I got older, I slowly began noticing the differences in my life: I spoke a second (uncommon) language, I didn't look the same as them, and, of course, I always had warm and extremely aromatic lunches that would not lose their smell no matter how many bags and jumpers I wrapped them in!

My mother, Kamila Darweish, born in Zanzibar in 1960, moved to the UK in 1965, pictured above (and above right in 1998).

Dina Macki (me!), born in the UK in 1994, pictured above and above left with Mum.

My father, Mahmood Abdul Nabi Macki, born in Oman in 1940.

Bibi, my maternal grandmother, Hashum Abdul-Hussein (right), born in Zanzibar in 1938, pictured above with Babu.

Babu, my maternal grandfather, Mohammed Darweish, born in Zanzibar in 1928.

My maternal great-uncle (Gigi), Jamshid Abdul-Hussein (right), born in Zanzibar in 1936.

Bibi's parents, Abdul Hussein & Umukheir. Abdul Hussein was half Iranian and half Zanzibari and East African. Umukheir (also known as Bibi Wa Kati, "the middle grandmother") was born and raised in Muscat to Omani parents, and moved to Zanzibar at the age of 10 for a better life.

During the summer holidays, we would go to Oman. I always loved my time there, visiting family and playing with my many cousins. My cousins loved the fact I had a British accent and lived in England, and although I just wanted them to see me as one of them and not an outsider, I appreciated that I didn't have to hide any part of me. But it was never a trip I would get excited to tell my school friends about. All I wanted to do was visit countries they were familiar with. Growing up, I struggled to tell my friends that my family were from Oman and Zanzibar. Back then, they seemed like two completely unknown countries. I decided my best option was to say I was from Dubai, which at the time felt fitting, as the city had just begun to boom and was the talk of the town. Making this claim helped me fit in and feel more accepted. Reflecting 14 years later, I wish more than anything that I had told them I am Omani, and this is Oman.

I must have been at university when I really began to understand the details of Oman. My Arab friends at uni had grown up in the Middle East, and they poetically weaved Arabic words with English as they spoke about certain similarities shared between their respective countries, from childhood *khaleeji* snacks (*khaleeji* is an Arabic word describing people from the Gulf), to national anthems that were sung every day at assembly. They swapped stories about the many weddings and funerals they attended every week thanks to their small communities where everyone knew each other. I would quietly observe, laughing when it seemed appropriate, and spending the rest of the conversation racking my brains trying to remember all the trips I had taken to Oman as a kid, as well as stories my mum would tell me about her time there, just so I could come up with something to say and feel like I belonged.

In my quest to fit in with my new friends, I turned to my love for food, and delved into Omani cuisine on my journey to discover where I was "really from" and who I actually am. It turns out that every bowl of ingredients I mix together, every meal I plate up and every bite I take leads me on an adventure through family trees and maritime history. Most importantly, my constant cooking teaches me that the food I grew up eating is not alien, but a mix of me, my family, my heritage and the two countries beyond the UK that I refer to as home – Oman and Zanzibar. Now, I am happy to say that the aroma of freshly cooked rice, which I once considered a curse, is a true blessing: the smell of home.

Finding Home

In the summer of 2013, I had my first Ramadan without Bibi and my mother – or their cooking. I began to learn our recipes, with the help of FaceTime. I'd call them with a barrage of cooking questions: "How do you make *sambusa* (samosa)?"; "How do you do that rice with those little red things?"; "How can I tell when my lamb is cooked?"

The challenge in all of this was that I was fasting and couldn't even taste-test, so had to rely on my housemates' tastes. But somehow, with the guidance of Bibi and my mum, we did it. Little by little, my memories of being with Bibi in the kitchen resurfaced, along with the recollections of the house I'd grown up in. As I recreated all the scents I had once tried to shed, my new appreciative and hungry uni friends were embracing my food all around me. They showed up for me and for my culture. And that's when I realised that this food, the cuisine of my heritage, is who I am. I was finally and proudly introducing myself as an Omani. I began spending all my nights cooking and baking, and before long, whether it was Omani or not, I wanted to make it. I became obsessed with how people were reacting to my food and how their faces would light up when they took their first mouthful. I loved how the apartment became full of people eager to eat, reminding me of all the weekends our Omani-Zanzibari community came together in Portsmouth.

When I first had the idea for *Bahari*, I was determined to put Omani cuisine on the food map; my focus was all about showing the world how vast and varied Middle Eastern cuisine actually is, as well as wanting people to learn about the beauty of Oman. When I began writing, I planned to concentrate on recipes that were truly "Omani", but my naive unresearched self quickly came to learn that Oman's cuisine is so rich and beautiful precisely because it's a mix of so many incredible places and fascinating histories. Having now reached the end, I can wholeheartedly say that I was the perfect person to write this book. You see, as I travelled the whole country in search of recipes and stories, I came to learn of the completely different worlds in which the inhabitants of each region live, from the Bedouins in the desert to the lively communities of

the coastal cities. They all have their own foods and traditions, and generally seem uninterested in what is not theirs. To me, it seemed as if everyone was absorbed in their own Omani bubble. I was curious to learn about all their dishes, and so on I went, full of questions whose answers have made it into this book.

I have always sat alone at the table, so far removed from my Omani and Zanzibari heritage, yet yearning to be part of it; being brought up British, yet feeling like a foreigner in England. I guess like many third-culture kids, I can sometimes feel like I'm not from here, nor from there, and simply don't belong anywhere. *Bahari* and this food journey have become part of my quest for an identity, and have brought me a sense of belonging I once thought was unattainable. I am far away enough to see the nuances in Oman's culture, yet close enough to tell the story as if I am one of them. It's been a blessing in disguise to have this multitude of backgrounds, along with my lust for culture and fondness for home comforts. It's allowed me to bring *Bahari* to your table, along with a plethora of stories, history and hopefully new recipes that represent me and our people.

COOK'S NOTES

Growing up, the kitchen was always the centre of my family home, and there would always be food on the go. Because of this, a lot of the recipes in *Bahari* reflect my fondness for slow-cooking and spending time in the kitchen. In this book, you will find a mixture of traditional dishes, adaptations and very much "me" recipes. Many are for a whole meal, while others are smaller dishes to be served as part of a spread. All of them are made to bring people together around the table.

Where I can, I have tried to simplify recipes or suggest alternatives. The notes below are just to give you some guidance on what I use and why, but if you're confident in the kitchen, please do whatever you prefer – and just enjoy.

Garlic paste and garlic cloves

◆ I usually use garlic paste instead of fresh cloves. This is mainly because I've been brought up by women who don't like to waste time on things that can be done for them, so I like to use garlic paste to save time and effort. If you prefer to use fresh garlic, that's fine, but you will need to mash it into a paste in order to get the maximum flavour.
◆ If you buy garlic paste, make sure it is at least 90–99 per cent garlic. Go for the jars in the international aisle – they always are!
◆ If a recipe calls for fresh garlic, don't use paste – the intensity will be too much.

Chillies

◆ Whenever I mention fresh green or red chillies, I am referring to the small, skinny, bird's-eye chillies. These are easy to buy anywhere and tend to pack a lot of heat.
◆ All my recipes can be made without the chilli if you prefer.

Whole or ground spices?

◆ Please, for the sake of all your recipes, try grinding your own whole spices rather than buying them ready-ground! The flavour is unmatched and they are far more fragrant.
◆ Ground spices are usually kept in warehouses and shops for so long that they just become dusty and diluted in flavour.
◆ Whole spices retain their flavour and fragrance much better, and that will always come through in the dishes.

Dried Limes

◆ Dried limes are commonly used in Oman instead of fresh lemon. Nowadays, these can be found in larger supermarkets, as well as Mediterranean or Iranian stores.
◆ You'll either find dark yellow dried limes or black dried limes. Either type can be used in my recipes.
◆ The black version has been boiled in a salty brine before being dried out, so it has more depth to its flavour. I prefer this variety with beef dishes.

Tamarind block or paste?

- I am very pro using a tamarind block. It lasts longer, goes further, you get more value for your money and the flavour is much better.
- Using a tamarind block involves breaking some of it from the block and leaving it to soak in water until it can be turned into a pulp. This takes time and does involve the messiness of deseeding, but it gives you a brilliant base for any tamarind recipes.
- I do recommend paste from a bottle in a few recipes, because these dishes require a more concentrated flavour or such a small amount that it's not worth using the block.
- If you do prefer to use tamarind paste rather than a block, just remember that it will be heavily concentrated, so you may have to adjust the quantity.

Meat

- I opt for meat on the bone in a lot of my recipes, all because of the flavourful stock that comes from it.
- If you can't use meat on the bone, avoid supplementing this with stock cubes – I find they tend to mask the real flavour of the dish and instead create a standard salty stock flavour.
- If you are using boneless meat, the best way to bring out the flavour is through the spices in the dish, so don't be afraid to use more spice.

Salt

- I find salt the hardest ingredient to provide measurements for. I love my salt, but have really had to control how much I add in recipes. Please feel free to go with as much or as little salt as you prefer; it's all up to your taste on that one.
- If I just mention "salt", that means I am using table salt or fine sea salt.
- In certain recipes, and specifically in salads, I will mention "sea salt flakes"; using these will always make fresh dishes taste nicer. I find they don't go as far in cooked dishes, so you end up adding more, which is why I use finer salts there.

Oil

- When it comes to deep-frying, I have given an idea of how deep the oil should be, but the quantity of oil you need will depend on the size of your saucepan. I tend to suggest making the oil deep enough that whatever you are cooking will not touch the bottom when frying.
- When deep-frying in hot oil, the easiest way to check if the oil is hot enough is to drop a little of the batter (or whatever you are frying) into the oil. If it sizzles straight away, that's a good indication that the oil is ready.

If you travel across the whole of Oman, you'll soon notice how vastly different the capital's food culture is to the rest of the country. While tourists and people from Muscat assume the recipes they eat here are eaten all over Oman, the truth is they are not. Muscat's cuisine captures the impact of migration, merchants and maritime history, drawing together all the flavours of tamarind, dried limes, hibiscus, lemons and pomegranates. Before I started living with my father's side of the family as an adult, I was absorbed in the Zanzibari and Swahili influences of my mother's family, but I soon grew fascinated with the array of recipes brought from the Balochi, Lawati and Bahrani families, as well as the residents of the old town, Mutrah.

Auntie Dalia's Mutahfy

Salmon, Tamarind & Aubergine Curry

Serves 3–4

500g (1lb 2oz) salmon fillets or
    tuna steaks, skin removed,
    cut into small cubes
2 heaped tsp ground cumin
2 heaped tsp ground cinnamon
2 heaped tsp ground coriander
2 heaped tsp freshly ground
    black pepper
1 heaped tsp ground turmeric
1 tsp salt
240g (8½oz) tamarind block
350ml (1½ cups) plus 1 tbsp
    vegetable oil
1 onion, thinly sliced
2 aubergines (eggplants), sliced
    into 1cm (½in) rounds
1 tbsp garlic paste
1 tbsp ginger paste
2 green chillies, sliced
3 tbsp tomato purée (paste)
400g (14oz) can chopped
    tomatoes
handful of fresh coriander
    (cilantro), roughly chopped
crispy dried onions, to garnish
    (optional)

Mutahfy is eaten by people who are originally from Muscat, usually Shia Muslims who grew up by the Mutrah Corniche. The sauce base is so full of flavour that you can make it without fish as a vegan dish. I sometimes serve it like this as a dip, too. Traditionally, it is made with tuna, so if you live somewhere with delicious fresh tuna, please go for that! I usually serve this with white basmati rice.

In a large bowl, combine the salmon or tuna with 1 heaped teaspoon of each of the ground spices, along with the salt. Stir well, then cover and leave to marinate in the fridge for at least 1 hour.

In a separate bowl, soak your tamarind block in 400ml (1¾ cups) of warm water for at least 1 hour until the seeds have separated and the water has diluted the tamarind into a pulp. Strain the pulp through a colander to remove the seeds, making sure you don't lose any of the liquid! It should have quite a thin consistency; if not, add a bit more water.

When you're ready to cook, combine 250ml (1 cup plus 1 tbsp) of the oil with the onion in a medium-sized saucepan (starting from room temperature rather than heating the oil first). Place over a high heat and fry for 15 minutes until golden.

Meanwhile, arrange the aubergine slices in a frying pan and pour over the remaining 100ml (scant ½ cup) of oil – it should be enough to almost cover them. Again, we're starting at room temperature. Place the pan over a high heat and fry for 5–10 minutes on each side until golden in the middle and turning slightly black at the edges (the second sides will cook faster). Transfer to a plate lined with kitchen paper (paper towels) to soak up the excess oil, and set aside until needed.

Once the onion is nice and golden, add the garlic and ginger paste, followed by the chillies, tomato purée and canned tomatoes. Stir to combine, then leave to cook for about 5 minutes. Add three-quarters of the aubergine slices and stir to combine, slightly mashing them as you stir. Now stir in the tamarind liquid, along with all the remaining spices. Leave to simmer over a medium heat for 15 minutes until the stew thickens.

Remove your fish from the fridge. Heat the 1 tablespoon of oil in a frying pan over a medium heat, then add the fish and fry for 2 minutes on each side until it is sealed and slightly crispy and golden on the outside. Add the fish to the curry mix, stir and leave to simmer for a further 5 minutes (or up to 10 minutes if you're using tuna).

Before serving, stir in the fresh coriander, along with a little water to loosen if needed. Serve topped with the reserved aubergine slices and some crispy fried onions, if you like.

THE BALOCHI & LAWATI QABAYEL IN OMAN

I've always loved the concept of having your family, and then your *qabeela*. The sense of affiliation to a wider community has always made me feel protected. In the spirit of preserving cultural nuances and authenticity, I use the Arabic word *qabeela* throughout this book to convey a deeper sense of identity and community. *Qabeela* (plural *qabayel*) translates into English as "tribe", but it holds much more significance to Omanis and other Gulf countries than the simple translation. It encapsulates the essence of unity, shared traditions and, perhaps most importantly, a strong sense of belonging – something I have searched for all my life, having grown up away from my culture. We use our *qabeela* as our family name, and understanding *qabayel* allows us to see how we can be connected to someone else. It also provides us with a sense of protection, community and support. While the term "tribe" can sometimes carry negative connotations and suggest notions of separation, *qabeela* reflects the warmth and communal nature that underlies the culinary experiences shared within these pages.

The luck of having such a small population in Oman has meant we are able to easily trace our *qabayel* and work out who is related to whom. There are around 200 *qabayel* in Oman, with each coming from a

specific village or having a particular ethnic ancestry. We are so in tune with our *qabayel* that among friends, we can joke about certain habits or characteristics each has, and we can also instantly tell who is from which *qabeela* just by looking at someone's features. I always remember my mum and Bibi referring to people by their *qabeela*, but it wasn't until I was in my late teens and began taking more trips to Oman that I started to understand the nuances and stigmas, and the impact they have on society. Although it's not as bad today, people will naturally ask what your *qabeela* is. This is usually just out of curiosity, but older generations and some people from interior areas may use it to steer the conversation and build their understanding of you. To them, your *qabeela* helps to give a generalised understanding of your background and habits.

While so many of these *qabayel* are impactful or well known in the country, the two that always bring much conversation – especially when it comes to comparing recipes –are the Al Balochi and Al Lawati families from Muscat. As you drive down to Mutrah Corniche, one of the first buildings you see on your left is a prominent period building with a white and turquoise façade. The house is very picturesque; if you search online for "Mutrah blue house", you'll see it in the search results. Similar in architectural style to typical houses from Old Muscat and Zanzibar's capital, Stone Town, this home sits regally at the beginning of the Corniche as if it belonged to a royal family member. Inside live two elderly Lawati sisters, who have lived there their whole lives, and also happen to be my friend Abdullah's aunties and the grandmothers to some of my cousins. To them, it is simply their home, in the area in which Lawati families grew up: a district known as Sur Al Lawatia, which used to be closed off to the public, earning it the name "the forbidden city". No one really knows why it was closed off; it was always their domain, and nobody questioned it. Now, everyone is free to walk through the alleys, which transport you to another era as you pass the antiquated houses.

Both my mother and father's families came from Old Muscat and Mutrah. It was predominantly a Shia Muslim area, and their community mosque and *matam* (community space) are still the place where our *qabayel* congregate for prayers, weddings and religious gatherings. If you ever visit Mutrah Corniche, the most serene moment of each day is when the minarets of the mosque fill the port with a harmonious call to prayer (*adhan*), as the sun glares out across the *bahari* (ocean), the seagulls croon and the fishermen prepare their boats for the next morning.

Our links to Mutrah stem from our *qabeela* ties to Bahrain, while the Lawatis' roots reach back to India and Iran, prior to settling in Oman hundreds of years ago. One particular area they were known to come from was Sindh, a province that is now part of Pakistan, bordering the south of Balochistan. The relationship between Balochistan and Oman dates back to the fourth millennium BCE, thanks to trade links with Makran (the name for coastal Balochistan back then) and Mesopotamia. These links were established again in the 17th century during the Yaruba dynasty, and have continued through to the current Al Said dynasty. Since the early days of Islam (1,400 years ago), Balochis were nomadic, until the majority began to settle in Muscat and down the Batinah coast of Oman. The Yaruba dynasty established a lot of commercial influence, which stretched across the Persian Gulf to the starting point of the Ganges river in India. It wasn't till 1797 that Gwadar (in Balochistan) became part of the Sultanate of Muscat and Oman, and then in 1958, following negotiations, it was handed over to Pakistan. The trade and political links between the two countries meant that during the 19th century, many Balochis joined Oman's military, particularly the special forces.

Over the last hundred years, Balochis were able to settle in Oman and eventually call it home, with most of them coming to Muscat, as it was the closest point to Balochistan.

Paplouh

Balochi/Lawati Lemon
Swordfish Soup

Serves 3–4

1 tbsp garlic paste
2 onions, finely diced
2 green chillies, roughly chopped
2 tomatoes, quartered
½ tsp ground coriander
1 tbsp ground turmeric
650g (1lb 7oz) swordfish or
    alternative, chopped into small
    chunks
salt, to taste
juice of 1–2 lemons, to taste
small bunch of coriander
    (cilantro), about 30–40g
    (1–1½oz), finely chopped

With Lawatis and Balochis being so close in terms of heritage, it is no wonder that they overlap on recipes – and those living alongside one another in the city are engaged in a never-ending debate over who does it better. One particular recipe they may never agree on is the making of a fish soup called *paplouh* (pronounced "bab-low"). My cousins are married into Lawati families, while I have many friends from Balochi families, and both sides are always confident that their version is the best. *Paplouh* is a turmeric and lemon soup made with either kingfish or tuna pieces, relying heavily on the stock of the fish for flavour. Although it has the consistency of a soup, we usually eat it like a curry, placing rice in a bowl and then pouring *paplouh* over it until it's practically swimming. Having now eaten plenty of *paplouh*, I've come to realise that most Lawatis really strip back what goes into the dish. One of my in-laws, Zahra, always tells me a real *paplouh* should only have fish, turmeric, lemon, onion and fresh chilli. Meanwhile, my Balochi friend Farah has always made it with lots of lemon, a tomato (which shouldn't be cut up too much, or it will change the colour) and some fresh coriander, added just before serving. While I happily eat both versions with no complaints, I much prefer the Balochi way thanks to the added acidity and the freshness of the coriander – but let's not tell my family that! Regardless of who makes it best, this will always be a comforting dish to have. Even when Oman is in 40°C (104°F) heat, we will still ask for it at lunch. The relationship between the fish stock, onions and lemon is a beautiful one.

In a large saucepan, combine 1.5 litres (6¼ cups) of water with the garlic paste, onions, chillies, tomatoes, ground coriander and turmeric. Place over a medium–high heat and bring to the boil.

Once it begins to bubble, add the fish. Stir, then leave the mixture to gently simmer over a medium heat for about 10 minutes, until the fish is cooked through. Add the salt and lemon juice, to taste, then reduce the heat to low and continue to simmer for another 15 minutes.

When you're ready to eat, stir through the fresh coriander and serve.

Qashod

Spiced Prawn & Turmeric Dumplings with Honey Chilli Oil

Serves 3–4

4 tbsp olive oil, plus 2 tsp for frying
1 small onion, finely chopped
1 tsp garlic paste
1 tsp ginger paste
2 tsp baharat spice blend (see page 120)
1 tsp ground turmeric
1 tbsp chilli flakes (optional, if you like heat)
3 tsp ground dried lime
400g (14oz) fresh or frozen baby prawns, finely chopped
3 tbsp tomato purée (paste)
½ tsp salt
15g (½ oz) coriander (cilantro), finely chopped
10g (¼ oz) dill, finely chopped

For the honey chilli oil
1 garlic clove, finely chopped
1 heaped tbsp chilli flakes
7 tbsp runny honey
2 red chillies, roughly chopped
1 tbsp neutral oil, such as light vegetable oil

For the dumpling wrappers
200g (generous 1½ cups) plain (all-purpose) flour, plus extra for dusting
1 tsp ground turmeric
pinch of salt

I first saw this recipe in the handwritten recipe book belonging to my Auntie Munira, my father's sister. The concept of this dish was confusing at first; it uses similar methods to a curry but has a very different consistency. It's thick and has very little excess liquid, so it's rather like a pâté. Luckily, a good friend, Abdullah, who happens to adore cooking, comes from the Al Lawati *qabeela* (see page 22). Although they have their own dishes unique to their community, there are some overlaps with cuisines of other *qabayel*, including *qashod*. Abdullah taught me how to make it one winter when we were cooking at a hotel in Salalah, and explained that the dish's thick texture was originally intended to make it easier to transport on long journeys.

The dish is usually made with tuna, but I have opted for prawns (much to Abdullah's disapproval and confusion), as tuna in the UK just isn't as tasty. I also decided to make the prawns into dumplings; to me, this felt like a natural evolution of the dish. You can always opt for fresh tuna if you are able to source it; this would bring you closer to an authentic *qashod*. I finish the dish with a hot honey and chilli drizzle, which adds the perfect accent.

Begin by making the honey chilli oil. Add all the ingredients to a small saucepan, along with 2 tablespoons of water, and heat very gently over a low temperature for about 10 minutes. You are waiting for the honey to become thinner and begin to bubble slightly around the sides of the pan. You don't want it piping hot. Set aside to cool.

Heat 4 tablespoons of the oil in a large frying pan over a high heat. Add the onion, and the garlic and ginger pastes, along with all the spices and the ground lime, and fry for about 5 minutes, stirring until everything is well incorporated.

Reduce the heat to medium–high and add the prawns, tomato purée and salt. Fry for 5 minutes until all the liquid has evaporated and the mixture is dry. Be sure to keep stirring so nothing burns or sticks.

Add the coriander and dill and briefly mix them in, cooking for no more than a minute. We want the herbs to stay as fresh as possible. Set the mixture aside to cool.

To prepare the dumpling wrappers, you'll need 110–130ml (scant–generous ½ cup) of very warm water. I achieve this by combining three parts boiling water with one part room-temperature water.

Recipe continues overleaf

In a mixing bowl, combine the flour, turmeric and salt. Add the warm water slowly, a little at a time, using a fork to cut it through. You will certainly need at least 110ml (scant ½ cup); depending on your flour, you may not need the rest, so only add it if you feel your dough is not coming together.

Start to bring the mixture together with your hands, then transfer to a lightly floured surface and knead for about 10 minutes until your dough is super soft (if you like, you can do this in a mixer instead).

Once the dough is soft and smooth, place it in a lightly floured bowl and cover with a damp cloth. Leave it to rest for at least 30 minutes, but remember: the longer it rests, the better.

After resting, knead the dough briefly, then make a hole in the middle and start to create a big ring. You want the dough to be about 2.5cm (1in) thick. Slice the ring into 16 pieces; each should weigh about 10g (¼oz). Roll the pieces into round balls, then roll them around on a floured surface to coat.

Take the first ball and flatten it with the palm of your hand, then start rolling it out with a rolling pin, turning it each time you roll so that the dough thins out evenly. Once you have gone all the way round, start rolling the edges only, so the middle stays slightly thicker. Set aside on a floured surface and repeat with the rest of the dough balls.

To make the dumplings, take a heaped teaspoon of the prawn filling and place it in the middle of one of the wrappers. Bring one edge of the wrapper across to form a semicircle. To seal the sides, either pinch all the way around or pleat them like a fan, by folding the edges over each other. Repeat with the remaining wrappers and filling. Keep the wrappers covered with a clean tea towel as you work so the dough doesn't dry out.

Heat the 2 teaspoons of oil in a non-stick frying pan over a medium–high heat. Add your dumplings, arranging them flat-side down, and leave to fry for about 2 minutes until they brown and crisp up on the bottom. Then add 50ml (scant ¼ cup) of water to the pan, cover with a lid and leave to steam for exactly 6 minutes.

Drizzle the dumplings with the honey chilli oil before serving.

Cornflake "Fried" Cod

Serves 2

2 cod loin steaks, about
500g (1lb 2oz)

For the marinade
1 tsp onion powder
½ tsp ground ginger
½ tsp garlic powder
2 tsp lemon juice
1 tsp ground cumin
2 tbsp neutral oil, such as light
vegetable oil, plus extra for
drizzling
1 tsp chilli powder

For the coating
50g (1¾oz) cornflakes, roughly
crushed
30g (1oz) cornflour
1 large egg, beaten

When my mum lived in Oman, she worked for the Royal Oman Police within their Royal Flight division. She loved her time there, and it was actually how she met my father. You know, one of those classic love stories: girl meets boy on a plane. She tells me that every Friday, they would have either cornflake chicken or fish at the Police Club, a members' club for those in the police force. Her fond memories of her time there meant I had to eat a lot of cornflake chicken and fish in my childhood! I love both, but I always remember her telling me this cornflake fish was her version of the classic battered cod. So, here is her recipe. It works well in an air fryer too! You can use the same marinade and coating for chicken if you prefer.

In a shallow bowl, mix together all the ingredients for the marinade, then add the fish loins and turn in the marinade to coat. Leave to marinate for at least 1 hour, or overnight in the fridge.

When you're ready to cook, preheat your oven to 200° C (180° C fan/400° F/Gas 6) and line a baking tray with baking parchment (parchment paper).

For the coating, place the cornflakes, cornflour and beaten egg into three separate bowls.

Take the first cod loin and coat in the cornflour, then dip in the egg, making sure it is completely coated. Dip in the cornflakes to coat, then repeat with the second loin.

Place the coated cod on the baking tray, drizzle with a little oil and bake for around 12 minutes until cooked through. I enjoy serving this with some sautéed veg or chunky fries.

Kubba Curry

Smoked Haddock
Kebab Curry

Serves 4

For the sour curry
7 tbsp olive oil or vegetable oil
1 onion, finely diced, peel reserved
1 tsp garlic paste
1 lsp ginger paste
400g (14oz) can chopped
    tomatoes
2 tbsp tomato purée (paste)
1 tbsp mild curry powder
1 green chilli, finely chopped
2 dried limes, pierced
2 bay leaves

For the haddock kebabs
1 small onion, roughly chopped,
    peel reserved
1 tsp ginger paste
1 tsp garlic paste
1 tsp freshly ground black pepper
1 tsp ground cumin
1 tsp ground fenugreek
½ tsp chilli powder
1 small green or red chilli
25g (scant 1oz) coriander (cilantro)
juice of 1 small lemon
salt, to taste
625g (1lb 6oz) haddock fillets, skin
    removed
1 egg

Flameproof wire rack
Natural wood charcoal
Lighter or gas hob

This recipe came about when I was trying to make fish kebabs; I had already begun making the mixture when I realised I was missing half the ingredients! I remember learning from a cousin's cook in Oman how to smoke your fish so that it binds together, so I followed her instructions and the kebabs held. Although they were delicious on their own, I felt they needed more body, so the addition of a sour curry was the perfect way forward. Haddock is my favourite fish for this recipe, but you can use tuna, cod or sea bass. Serve with rice.

For the curry sauce, heat the oil in a large saucepan over a medium–high heat. Add the onion and fry for 10–12 minutes until golden brown. Add the garlic and ginger pastes and stir to combine, then add all the other curry ingredients, along with 200ml (scant 1 cup) of water. Bring to the boil, then reduce the heat to low. Leave to simmer while you prep the fish. (This sauce can be made in advance, and doing so will yield a more intense sour flavour from the dried limes.)

To make the kebabs, mince the onion in a food processor, then transfer to a strainer and squeeze out all the liquid. Return the squeezed onion to the food processor and add all the other kebab ingredients except the fish and egg . Blend well until everything is finely chopped and combined.

Add the fish and pulse to combine, making sure the fish breaks up but doesn't turn to paste. Now break in the egg and use your hands to massage it into the mixture. Transfer to the fridge and leave to rest for at least an hour.

When you're ready to cook, use your hands to roll the mixture into golf-ball-sized balls; you should be able to make about 12.

Now prepare your smoker on the hob. First, take a flameproof wire rack that will fit in a wide frying pan or wok. Cover it with foil and place the fish balls on top, then set aside until needed. Arrange some large pieces of the reserved onion peel in the bottom of the pan or wok, then place the pan over a medium heat (if you have a gas hob, use a low–medium heat).

Burn your charcoal with a lighter so it begins smoking (if you have a gas hob, you can use this flame), then place on top of the onion peel. Working quickly, take the wire rack containing the fish balls and place it on top of the charcoal, then cover with a lid to capture the smoke. Leave to smoke for about 6–8 minutes, or until the smoke stops.

Carefully add the smoked fish balls to the curry and cook, still over a low heat, for at least 10 minutes. If the curry has thickened a lot, add a splash of water to loosen. Serve with rice.

Silqa

Hake, Dried Lime &
Thyme Curry

Serves 4

1 onion, thickly sliced
1 cinnamon stick
1 tomato, quartered
½ tsp ground cinnamon
1 tsp garlic paste
1 tsp ginger paste
½ tsp ground turmeric
150g (5½oz) new potatoes, halved
1 dried lime, pierced
1 green or red chilli, left whole or
    halved (optional)
2 tbsp tomato purée (paste)
450g (1lb) hake, cut into circular
    pieces with bone in the middle
1 tbsp dried thyme, or 3 fresh
    thyme sprigs

Never did I think such an easy dish could cause so many problems when attempting to cook it in another country! In developing this recipe, I must have spent a ridiculous amount of money on fish. *Silqa* comes from Muscat, and isn't really known outside of the capital. At my cousin Hilal's house, they make it at least once a week. Traditionally, it's made with tuna, which my cousin's chef would pick up fresh from Mutrah fish market in the morning. Although I've called it curry here, it has more of a soup-like texture, and I like to drown my rice in it when eating. While trying to get this recipe right for *Bahari*, I first tested it with tuna and it was a disaster – there was absolutely zero flavour, as the quality of the tuna available in the UK simply isn't as good. So I started testing it with every other fish possible, and surprisingly, hake was the answer. Usually, you would use dried za'atar leaves instead of thyme, but thyme is easier to find outside of Oman and is a perfect substitute. If you live in a country that has fresh tuna, please do use it; likewise, if you are able to get dried za'atar leaves, please use them. Serve with white rice.

In a large saucepan, combine all the ingredients except the fish and thyme. Add 1 litre (4⅓ cups) of water and bring to the boil over a high heat. Once boiling, leave to cook for 25 minutes until reduced and ever so slightly thicker.

Add the fish pieces and remove the dried lime, then reduce the heat to medium and leave to simmer for a further 20 minutes.

Add the thyme and stir through, then simmer for a final 5 minutes. The mixture should be soup-like in consistency. Serve in a pasta bowl with rice, slightly drowning the grains in the *silqa*.

DRIED LIMES

When life gave our culture and my family lemons, we made sure to use them in every single marinade, chutney, drink and home remedy – we even use them to clean our hands after we've eaten a piquant-smelling fish. Despite Oman's arid climate, we produce a bountiful supply of lemons. Our lemons are rather cute and dainty; not your typical bold, oval and slightly wrinkled sunshine-yellow lemon, but more of a round, lime-like shape, delicate and thin-skinned, in tones of pear green and Parmesan yellow. Their flavour is like a typical lemon, but with sweet undertones of lemon grass leaves and green apples. Thanks to their appearance, they are often referred to as limes.

Oman's biggest claim to fame comes from how we learned to preserve this versatile fruit and give them a second lease of life as a pungent dried lime known across the world as Omani *loomi,* or

as *limoo/limu Omani* (*limoo* meaning "lemon" in Farsi), or sometimes *loomi* or *noomi Basra.* I would say the dried lime has been Oman's only representation within the culinary world. I remember seeing a recipe in the Ottolenghi book *Flavour* that mentioned Omani *loomi,* and I was over the moon to see Oman's name next to a fruit in a book that would have been read by millions. To me, they had made Oman famous in one simple recipe. At the time, that was all the representation I needed. Dried limes have been made in Oman since it was a part of the Assyrian empire, and they were traded with neighbouring countries, but the great minds who made the ingredient famous in modern times were my father's uncles, Hussain, Dawood and Abdullah Hamza Al Asfoor. These three brothers were on a mission to grow enough *loomi* on their family farm to export it across the world, and, according to the narratives shared with me by my family, they were modern Oman's first *loomi* exporters. The majority of their business ended up coming from Iraq, which is how the name *loomi Basra* (Basra being a city in Iraq) came about. Unfortunately, my great uncles stopped

exporting when their lemon trees caught a disease that meant they all had to be destroyed. They were still proud to have been the pioneers for dried limes, and were happy to step back and leave others to continue producing them across the world.

The method for drying them remains the same today. Farmers and families will wash the limes by hand and then lay them out on their rooftops to dry in the sun. In the summer, they can easily be ready within a couple of days thanks to the seething heat, while in the winter months, it can take up to a week. Once dried, these limes can literally be stored for years. Families that make them for themselves will bag them up and store them in a dark place and use them when needed. You'll sometimes find black ones, which are slightly more intense in flavour, and I tend to find they are better for grinding down to a powder. This black colour comes from boiling the fruits in salt water and then washing them in vinegar before they are dried out.

Patience and a gentle simmer are always the best approach for this ingredient; one good-quality *loomi* goes a long way in a recipe, and releases its flavour gently over time, so I always find the taste really intensifies and becomes powerfully tart and fragrant the morning after I've made something with it. Breaking the *loomi* shell is one way to speed up the process, but be careful, as the seeds are bitter. *Loomi* makes a beautiful addition to stews, rice recipes, marinades, sorbets and drinks – *loomi* tea is a very common household drink in Oman and Bahrain.

Lamb Qabooli

Seven-spiced Lamb & Rice with Pomegranate Saffron Chickpeas

Serves 4

4 tbsp neutral oil, such as light vegetable oil
1 onion, finely sliced
2 tbsp garlic paste
1 tbsp ginger paste
1 tbsp coriander seeds
1 tbsp freshly ground black pepper
1 tbsp ground cumin
1 tbsp baharat spice blend (see page 120)
1 tbsp cardamom pods
1 tbsp cloves
6 bay leaves
2 cinnamon sticks
2 dried limes, pierced
4 lamb shanks
salt, to taste

For the saffron infusion
1 tsp saffron threads
1 tbsp granulated sugar

For the rice and chickpeas
140g (1 cup) raisins or barberries
2 onions, finely sliced
5 tbsp neutral oil, such as vegetable oil
1 tbsp baharat spice blend
600g (3 cups) rice
400g (14oz) can of chickpeas
50g (1¾oz) cashews
3 tbsp pomegranate molasses
handful of freshly chopped coriander (cilantro) and pomegranate seeds, to garnish

Legend has it that this recipe originated from the city of Kabul, in Afghanistan. Omanis tell me stories of how Afghani travellers visiting to trade their food crops for our raw materials, such as copper, would cook their version of *Kabuli pulao* for the locals. Over the years, the dish has been adapted to include spices brought from India, Iran and Zanzibar. *Qabooli* is served at local restaurants across the country, either on its own, or with fish, lamb, chicken, goat or even camel. I often make the rice on its own, as it brings life and vibrancy to any table. It's no more difficult to cook than plain rice, and for me it's the easiest way to bring a piece of Oman into my home.

For this recipe, I've used lamb shanks, mainly because they are my favourite. When I have many guests to feed, I will use a leg or shoulder of lamb, grinding the spices and making a paste to coat the meat, then wrapping it well and roasting for 4–5 hours. Although you won't get any stock if you go for this method, you will have the extra roasting juices, so make sure to drizzle those over the top when serving.

Begin by preparing the saffron infusion. Using a pestle and mortar, pound the saffron strands and sugar until they form a powder, then transfer to a bowl or jug and pour over 500ml (generous 2 cups) of boiling water.

Place the raisins or barberries for the rice in a separate bowl and pour over 250ml (1 cup plus 1 tbsp) of the saffron infusion. Leave to soak, reserving the rest of the saffron infusion for the lamb.

Heat 4 tablespoons of the oil in a large saucepan over a medium heat. Add the onion, along with the garlic and ginger paste. Fry for a few minutes until the onion begins to sweat and become transparent, then add all the spices and the dried limes. Increase the heat to high and fry the spices and onions together for 2–3 minutes until everything has turned golden.

Make a couple of slits in each lamb shank, then lay them in the saucepan. Allow the shanks to brown on the bottom, then turn over to brown the other side. Make sure there is enough oil in the pan so that they don't burn or stick. Once you are happy with the colouring of your shanks, add about 1 litre (4⅓ cups) of water to the saucepan; it should just cover the shanks, so you may need a little more or less. Season with salt, then cover with the lid and leave to boil over a high heat for 1 hour.

After an hour, check on the lamb. The shanks will have shrunk considerably and the meat should be coming away from the bone. Taste the liquid for seasoning and add more salt if required, then cover and cook for a further 25 minutes.

Recipe continues overleaf

Preheat the oven to 180° C (160° C fan/350° F/Gas 4) and line a roasting tray with foil.

Now get started on the rice. Add one of the onions to a medium-sized saucepan, along with 1 tablespoon of the oil and the baharat. Fry over a medium heat for 4–5 minutes until golden, then add the rice and stir to combine. Set aside.

By this point, your lamb will be ready for roasting. Carefully lift the lamb shanks out of the saucepan and place them on the prepared roasting tray. Brush the reserved saffron water all over them to glaze. Cover with a second piece of foil, making sure it's sealed all around, then roast for 45 minutes.

Meanwhile, pour 1 litre (4⅓ cups) of the stock from the lamb over your rice (if you're not a fan of whole spices in your food, you can use a sieve to catch them as you pour). Cover with a lid and leave the rice to cook over a low heat for 20–25 minutes until all the liquid is absorbed and the rice is soft and fluffy.

Heat the remaining 4 tablespoons of oil in a frying pan over a medium heat and add the remaining onion. Fry for a few minutes until it begins to turn golden, then add the saffron-soaked dried fruit. Stir in the chickpeas and cashews, followed by the pomegranate molasses, and fry for 5 minutes until the nuts have slightly softened.

Once everything is ready, divide the rice between plates, then top with the chickpea mix, followed by the roasted lamb shanks. Scatter over the chopped coriander and pomegranate seeds to serve.

Fish Qabooli

Spiced Bream & Rice

Serves 6

2 whole sea breams, about
   450–500g (1lb–1lb 2oz)
2½ onions, thinly sliced
75g (2 ½ oz) cashew nuts, whole
75g (2 ½ oz) dried cranberries
8 tbsp vegetable oil
2 tbsp garlic paste
1 tbsp ginger paste
8 cardamom pods
2 cinnamon sticks
6 bay leaves
1 tbsp cloves (optional)
1 tbsp dried chilli flakes
1 tbsp coriander seeds
1 tbsp ground black pepper
1 tbsp ground cumin
3 tbsp baharat spice blend (see
   page 120)
3 whole dried limes, pierced
600g (3 cups) basmati rice, rinsed
400g (14oz) can of chickpeas
1 tsp saffron threads (a good
   pinch)
1 tbsp granulated sugar
handful of coriander (cilantro),
   chopped, to garnish
pomegranate seeds, to garnish

For the marinade
2 tsp ground dried limes
1 tbsp garlic paste
juice of 1 lemon
2 tbsp vegetable oil
1 tbsp baharat spice blend
1 tsp ground cinnamon
1 tsp ground ginger
1 tsp ground turmeric
salt, to taste

This is the fish version of my Lamb Qabooli (see page 39), although the method is quite different. I've used whole fish, but you could easily make this with fillets. I really enjoy this version, as I love the flavour that comes from the combination of spices with the grilled skin of the fish.

Begin by combining all the marinade ingredients in a bowl. Mix well until you have a loose paste. In a large, shallow dish, coat both fish in the marinade. Stuff the fish with ½ onion and 30g (1oz) each of the cashews and cranberries, then place on a baking tray. Leave to marinate in the fridge for at least an hour.

When you're ready to cook, preheat the oven to 200° C (180° C fan/ 400° F/Gas 6).

Heat 5 tablespoons of the oil in a large saucepan over a high heat. Add 1 onion and fry for 8–10 minutes until translucent. Add the garlic and ginger pastes, cardamom, cinnamon, bay leaves, cloves, chilli flakes, coriander seeds, black pepper and cumin, along with 2 tablespoons of the baharat and the dried limes, then season with salt and fry for a further 5–10 minutes until the onion begins to brown.

Add the rice and stir through. Pour in 900ml (scant 4 cups) of water and increase the heat to high. Bring to the boil, then reduce the heat to very low. Securely wrap a tea towel around the saucepan lid and place on top to lock in the steam. Leave to cook for 20–25 minutes.

Meanwhile, cover the marinated fish with foil and bake in the oven for 25 minutes.

Heat the remaining 3 tablespoons of oil in a frying pan over a medium-high heat. Add the onion and remaining 1 tablespoon of baharat and sauté for 10 minutes until translucent. Add the chickpeas and remaining cashews, and fry for a further 2–3 minutes until the onion has browned.

Using a pestle and mortar, pound the saffron and sugar until they form a powder, then transfer into a bowl or jug and pour over 150ml (⅔ cup) boiling water. Pour this saffron infusion over the remaining cranberries in a bowl and leave to sit for at least 5 minutes, then tip this into the frying pan with the chickpeas and simmer for 6–7 minutes until all the liquid has evaporated.

Remove the foil from the fish and transfer to a grill set to a high heat. Grill for 5 minutes on each side to slightly crisp the skin and turn it golden brown. To serve, divide the rice between six plates, followed by the chickpea mixture. Scatter over the coriander and some of the pomegranate seeds, then top with the fish. Pour the juices of the fish over the top, then finish with more pomegranate seeds!

Mutrah Corniche Chutney Burger

Makes 8–9 patties

1 small red onion, roughly
  chopped
1 small sweet potato, peeled and
  roughly chopped
100g (3½oz) broccoli florets
1 tsp ground cumin
1 tsp freshly ground black pepper
salt, to taste
2–3 tbsp olive oil
215g (7½ oz) canned or jarred
  butter beans (drained weight)
100g (3½oz) jasmine rice
150g (5½oz) cashew nuts
25g (1oz) parsley, chopped
60g (½ cup) panko breadcrumbs
3 large eggs

For the chutney
30g (1oz) parsley
60g (2oz) coriander (cilantro)
20g (¾oz) mint leaves
juice of 2 lemons
2 hot green chillies
½–1 tsp sea salt

To serve (optional)
burger buns
your favourite fillings (I like
  lettuce and red onion slices)

Along the Corniche in Muscat is a little shop that appears from the outside to be selling drinks and snacks, but if you peer in, you'll notice that in the back left-hand corner, there's a chef cooking up his famous chutney burger. He's been around for at least 20 years, making the same thing. The 60p burger comes with a chicken patty and some salad, but it's the incredible chutney sauce that's the real draw for me. I make it a ritual to visit this place the minute I land in Muscat and again on the day I leave. I've tried many times to get the chutney recipe from him, and every time I visit, he reluctantly reveals one new ingredient. So this recipe took *many* trips – and *many* burgers – to figure out. Because for me it's all about the chutney, I decided a veggie burger would be best. So here is my own take on the best burger in Oman, but without the beautiful view of the Corniche.

Preheat the oven to 200°C (180°C fan/400°F/Gas 6) and line a baking tray with baking parchment (parchment paper).

Begin by combining the onion, sweet potato and broccoli in a food processor. Add the cumin and black pepper and season with salt, then whizz to chop the vegetables into small pieces, almost like big breadcrumbs. Tip this mixture on to one side of the prepared tray, then drizzle over 1 tablespoon of the olive oil and use your hands to mix through. Add the drained beans to the other side of the tray. Roast for 20 minutes until the vegetables begin to turn brown, then set aside to cool slightly.

In a saucepan, bring the jasmine rice to the boil with 300ml (1¼ cups) of water. Once boiling, reduce the heat to low and leave for 25 minutes until the water is fully absorbed and the rice is cooked through and fluffy.

Combine the cashews and parsley in the food processor and pulse slightly, then add the cooled vegetables and beans, along with the panko breadcrumbs and eggs. Pulse a few times to bring it together. Tip the mixture into a large bowl, along with the cooked rice. Use a spatula to fold in the rice until everything comes together. Transfer to the fridge for at least 30 minutes.

When you're ready to cook, separate your patty mixture into 8–9 balls, then press them flat; they should be just under 2.5cm (1in) thick. Heat the remaining 1–2 tablespoons of olive oil in a non-stick frying pan over a low–medium heat. Working in batches so as not to overcrowd the pan, fry the patties for 3–4 minutes on each side until brown and firm.

To make the chutney, simply blend all the ingredients together in a blender until smooth.

Assemble your burgers with your favourite buns and fillings; I usually just add onion and lettuce, as I don't want anything to overpower the chutney. You can also enjoy these patties naked, with just the sauce!

Omani Mishkak

Lamb Skewers with
Bergamot Syrup &
Tamarind Sauce

Makes 8

1 tbsp cumin seeds
4 tbsp coriander seeds
1 kiwi fruit, peeled
500g (1lb 2oz) lamb shoulder or
 leg, cut into 2.5cm (1in) cubes
2 tsp salt
1 heaped tsp garlic paste
1 heaped tsp ginger paste
2 tbsp vegetable oil, plus extra for
 brushing
tamarind sauce (see page 181),
 to serve

For the bergamot syrup (optional)

200g (1 cup) caster (superfine)
 sugar
½ bergamot, finely chopped,
 or 75g (2½oz) kumquats,
 thinly sliced

I remember one of my first ever trips to Oman when I was 11. My mum hadn't been back since I was born, and we were flying over for her adopted son's wedding. The night we arrived, we went to meet some of the family at Azaiba Beach, where hundreds of cars would flock when the sun had set. Bright headlights pierced the hazy air, which was filled with barbecue smoke. People had been coming to this spot for the last 20 years to buy fish and meat skewers from the same man. You could buy ten skewers for about £2.50. The only other offerings he had were tamarind sauce and chilli. On that first visit, my aunts huddled in the car with the AC blasting in their faces, while me, my mum and my brother sat outside, eating each skewer straight from the grill. Every trip to Oman after that, we made sure to pay a visit.

I started making my own version of these skewers for my dinner events at hotels in Oman. I wanted to bring locals something familiar, and tourists something traditional, but with more oomph.

The marinade I've used here is ever so simple, although I'd be confident in saying that the man selling skewers on the beach probably went simpler still, just adding a bit of garlic and allowing the sea salt breeze and charred coals to bring all the flavour. When cooked in an Omani's home, however, coriander seeds are key. The use of kiwi might seem unusual, but it is simply there to tenderise the meat (in Oman, we usually use green papaya). It works so well that you shouldn't really leave the kiwi on for longer than three hours, or your meat will fall apart on the grill – this has happened to me one too many times!

As well as the tamarind sauce, I've included an optional bergamot syrup for when you really want to impress. Many people don't realise this, but bergamot grows in Oman. It is known as *sfargel*, and is treated in the same way as lemon. I decided that we needed to give it more attention and created this syrup to celebrate it. If you want to try using fish instead of lamb, go for it. When I'm in Oman, I use camel.

Begin by making the syrup so that it has time to cool. Combine the sugar and bergamot or kumquats in a small saucepan with 250ml (1 cup plus 1 tbsp) of water and place over a high heat. Once it begins to bubble, leave it to boil vigorously for exactly 10 minutes, then reduce the heat to low–medium and leave to gently simmer for another 10 minutes. Remove from the heat and leave to cool.

To prepare the lamb, grind your cumin and coriander seeds using a pestle and mortar until fine.

In a blender, blend the kiwi to a fine pulp, then tip it into a large bowl. Add the lamb and massage the kiwi pulp into the meat. Add the ground spices and stir, then add the salt, garlic paste, ginger paste and oil. Stir to combine, ensuring the lamb is well coated.

Place in the fridge for at least 30 minutes, but no longer than 3 hours, as the kiwi will keep tenderising the meat until it falls apart.

When you're ready to cook, thread the lamb on to 8 skewers and place a griddle pan over a high heat or heat your barbecue to high. Brush the griddle or barbecue grill with oil, then place your skewers on top. If using a griddle pan, reduce the heat to medium and cover with a lid.

Cook for 5 minutes on one side before turning over and cooking on the other side for another 5 minutes.

Serve with the tamarind sauce and drizzle over the syrup, if using.

Basil &
Lime Ceviche

Serves 4

30g (1oz) basil
juice of 1½ limes
½ small red onion
4 cherry tomatoes
2 garlic cloves
1 celery stick
pinch of sea salt flakes
2 seabass fillets, about 180g
  (6¼oz), skin removed, cut into
  cubes or thin slices

To garnish (optional)
pomegranate seeds
edible flowers
thinly sliced pink radishes
fresh mango cubes

This was the first course at my first-ever supper club in Oman. The whole menu was inspired by Oman, but with the intention of bringing Western dishes to a city that lacks great international gastronomy. The supper club had been delayed by a year due to the Covid-19 pandemic, and I remember crying as if someone had died at the thought of disappointing my guests. I was so nervous that people wouldn't turn up the second time round, but we ended up going from 50 tickets to 150 tickets! To this day, I am in shock at how many people showed up for me: friends, family, followers and curious souls. This dish sums up the ethos of Dine with Dina; although very simple, it used Omani basil and limes with fresh Omani tuna, and spoke volumes about the food I create and want to bring to the table. I've used sea bass here, but if you can get hold of tasty fresh tuna, do use that.

In a blender, combine the basil, lime juice, onion, tomatoes, garlic, celery and salt, and blend together until smooth.

Using a muslin cloth or strainer, strain the mixture into a bowl until you are left with a clear green liquid. Add the fish to this liquid and place in the fridge to cure for at least 20 minutes, but no longer than 2 hours.

To serve, garnish as you like; I usually add fresh pomegranate seeds, edible flowers, thinly sliced pink radishes and tiny cubes of fresh, sweet mango.

Mum's Muhammara

Charred Red Pepper Dip

Serves 4–6

3 red (bell) peppers
3 tbsp date syrup, plus extra
    to serve
1 tbsp pomegranate molasses
75g (2½ oz) walnuts
1 tbsp olive oil
2 tsp ground cumin
1 tbsp dried chilli flakes
2 garlic cloves
sea salt, to taste

To garnish (optional)
freshly chopped parsley
pomegranate seeds
crushed walnuts

Muhammara is eaten across the whole of the Middle East. There are many versions out there, but my mum's muhammara is one of the best I've ever tasted. She doesn't do much differently to the traditional recipes, but when she started making it in Oman, she would add date syrup, and it became a "thing". That slight addition of rich, sticky sweetness brings something extra special to this dip.

Begin by charring your peppers over a flame until the skin is black and blistered. If you don't have a gas hob, you can do this in the oven: preheat to 220°C (200°C fan/425°F/Gas 7) and cook on a roasting tray for 15 minutes until charred, making sure to turn them over halfway.

Let the peppers cool, then peel off the skin and discard, along with the seeds. Add the flesh to a blender, along with all the remaining ingredients (except the garnishes). Blitz until everything is well blended and the walnuts have broken down to small, crumb-sized pieces. We don't want it to be completely smooth, as the walnuts add important texture.

Transfer to a plate or bowl and drizzle over some date syrup, then scatter over the garnishes and serve.

Mardhouf

Omani Date Paratha

**Makes 10 large breads or
16 small breads**

300g (10oz) dates, deseeded
725g (scant 5⅔ cups) plain
   (all-purpose) flour, plus extra
   for dusting
1 tsp salt
about 200g (7oz) warm ghee
250ml (1 cup plus 1 tbsp) coconut
   milk (optional – if you prefer, you
   can use room-temperature
   water instead)

We say date palms are the mother of our country, because every part of the date palm provides something for our families, including food and shelter, as well as cooking tools, rugs and baskets made from the palm fronds. Oman even has the Million Date Palm Plantation Project, which was created by our late Sultan, who believed that if the country ever came into hardship, the offerings of a date palm would save us. What I am trying to say is dates are so underrated: they are the ultimate superfood, and there are so many ways to use them outside of a cake or a smoothie. This bread is one of them.

This recipe is made by people from Muscat, mainly within the Bahraini Lawati *qabeela* (see page 22). I learned it from my dad's side of the family, and I rarely find it anywhere else except at their houses. For us, the layers are key, but if you're not feeling up to this extra step, they taste just as fabulous without. We have these for breakfast, drizzled with honey. We also enjoy them with savoury meals to add a subtle sense of sweetness, or just enjoy them on their own. Please note that the dates require soaking.

In a bowl, combine the dates with 250ml (1 cup plus 1 tbsp) of boiling water and leave to soak overnight or for a couple of hours to soften.

Once softened, use your hands to massage the dates until they break down into a pulp.

Either in a large bowl or a mixer, combine the flour, date pulp, salt and 3 tablespoons of the ghee with the coconut milk or room-temperature water. Mix the ingredients together by hand, or on a low speed if using a mixer, until the dough comes together in a ball. Now knead for 15–20 minutes by hand, or for 10 minutes on medium speed if using a mixer, until the dough is smooth and soft. Cover the bowl with cling film (plastic wrap) and leave to rest for 1 hour.

After the dough has rested, divide it into 10 balls (if you want large breads) or 16 (if you want smaller breads).

Take the first ball and roll it out as thinly as possible, ideally trying to keep it square, but don't worry too much about the shape at this stage. Sometimes, using your hands to stretch the dough is easier. If you are struggling to roll it thinly enough, spread a little warm ghee on your work surface and on the dough; this should help the dough to spread.

Once the dough is as thin as possible, drip 2 teaspoons of warm ghee on to the dough. Use your hands to spread it all around, making sure there are no dry parts.

Recipe continues overleaf

Now take the right-hand side of the dough and fold it into the middle. Then fold the left-hand side into the middle, leaving you with a rectangle. Next, fold the bottom of the rectangle into the middle, then fold the top into the middle. Flip it over, and you should be left with a neat square. Place this square on a plate and cover with cling film or a clean cloth. Repeat with the rest of the balls.

Once you have rolled and folded the dough into squares, you can create layers by repeating exactly the same process. You don't need to roll them out as thinly as the first time; you just need them to be big enough to fold. Roll out the first square, keeping the shape, and refold as above to create extra layers. Repeat with the remaining squares. You can skip this step if you don't want the extra layers.

Leave the dough squares to rest for at least 30 minutes, then heat a frying pan over a medium–high heat.

Take one dough square and roll it out, keeping the square shape, until it is about the thickness of a coin, then place it in the hot frying pan. Take 1 teaspoon of hot ghee and spread it around the edges of the dough. Allow the bread to fry slightly for 2 minutes, just enough so you can lift it with a spatula and flip it over, then take some more ghee and spread it around the edges on the other side. Press down on the edges of the dough with your spatula so they begin to fry well – we want the edges to be slightly crunchier, and the middle softer, which is why you spread the ghee on the edges first.

Now flip the bread once more and spread ghee all over it. Fry for 2–3 minutes, then flip again and spread ghee all over the other side – we don't want dry bread! Using your spatula, press down on the bread in the middle, rotating it in the pan at the same time, to make sure that it browns evenly all over. This will take about another 2–3 minutes. Flip once more and do the same on the other side. If the bread is browning too quickly or charring on the outside, reduce the heat.

Once you are happy that the paratha is fully browned and cooked through, transfer to a plate and repeat with the rest!

Serve with your chosen accompaniments. These breads will keep, wrapped in cling film in the fridge, for up to a week. They can also be frozen for up to a month and reheated in a frying pan with some ghee.

Khaliat Nahal

Honeycomb Bread

Makes 20 pieces

400ml (1¾ cups) + 2 tbsp
    warm milk
14g (scant ½ oz) fast-action dried
    yeast (2 packets)
650g (5¼ cups) plain (all-purpose)
    flour
130g (scant ¾ cup) caster
    (superfine) sugar
2 eggs
sesame seeds, for sprinkling
sea salt flakes

For the syrup
200g (1 cup) caster
    (superfine) sugar
2 tbsp runny honey
juice of ½ orange
4 cardamom pods, crushed

For the filling
200g (7oz) mozzarella
200g (7oz) soft cream cheese
    (I use Laughing Cow)

Qaranqasho is an Omani celebration that takes place on the 14th day of Ramadan, mainly across the north coast. Children dress up in traditional clothing and mothers prepare lots of nibbles and sweet baskets, then open up their doors to all. We call it Omani Halloween, where all the kids go "trick or treating" – but without the tricks! Everyone heads out after prayer time to visit friends, family and neighbours and collect sweets, little gifts and sometimes, if we're very lucky, money. I got to celebrate one Ramadan as a child in Oman, and I still remember the excitement as we ran through the streets, looking to see how many sweets we could collect.

Ramadan, specifically on Qaranqasho, is the only time of year you'll see *khaliat nahal*. My Auntie Nasra always made this bread instead of sweets. She'd set out whole trays of it on a table and wait for the children to run up, tear away their part and eat it on the go. Even as adults, we still want this bread at Ramadan; we know what's hidden inside, but there's still a joyful element of surprise. *Khaliat nahal* (which means "honeycomb") is a sweet, yeasted bread known for its honeycomb shape. This recipe is found in both Oman and Yemen; it's always filled with cheese, but the syrups drizzled over differ from family to family.

To make the syrup, combine all the ingredients in a saucepan with 170ml (scant ¾ cup) of water. Place over a high heat and bring to the boil. Once it starts bubbling, boil for exactly 10 minutes, then remove from the heat and leave to cool completely. Do not stir the syrup while it's boiling, and make sure it's entirely cool before you use it; the idea is to pour the cooled syrup over the hot bread.

Pour the 400ml (1¾ cups) milk into a bowl. Add the yeast and leave to sit for 5 minutes.

In a mixer or large bowl, combine the flour, sugar and eggs. Add the milk and yeast mixture, then combine. Knead until the dough is soft and smooth – this will take 10–12 minutes in a mixer, or 15–17 minutes by hand.

Cover with a clean damp cloth and leave to rise for 1½ hours or until it has doubled in size.

Recipe continues overleaf

Once risen, divide the dough into 20 even-sized pieces and shape into balls. Take the first ball and press it flat, then place a little mozzarella and soft cheese in the middle – just use about 5–10g (⅛–¼oz) of each, as you don't want to overfill. Bring the rest of the dough around the cheese to encase it, pinch the edges together to seal, then roll back into a ball and flatten very slightly. Repeat with the remaining dough balls and cheese.

Place the balls on a baking tray lined with baking parchment (parchment paper). Ideally, use a pizza tray, so you can arrange them in a honeycomb shape. Make sure to leave a little space between the balls so that they have room to spread as they rise.

Cover with a clean damp cloth and leave to rise for 30–45 minutes.

Preheat the oven to 200°C (180°C fan/400°F/Gas 6).

When the balls are ready to bake, brush them with the remaining 2 tablespoons of milk and sprinkle over the sesame seeds. Bake for 20–25 minutes until golden.

As soon as they come out of the oven, pour the cooled syrup over the top – or you can brush it on if you don't want too much. The syrup will seep into the dough. Sprinkle over some crushed sea salt flakes to finish.

Allow to cool for about 10 minutes, then serve while still warm so the cheese is melty and delicious. These are definitely best served freshly baked and warm, but will keep for 1–2 days in an airtight container.

Balochi Ice Cream

Buttermilk, Rose & Rambutan Ice Cream

Serves 5–6

200g (7oz) canned rambutans
3 egg yolks
75g (6 tbsp) caster
   (superfine) sugar
200ml (scant 1 cup) double
   (heavy) cream
3 tsp rose water
700ml (scant 3 cups) buttermilk

Back in the 1980s and 90s, you would find Balochi women sitting outside their houses in Muscat, selling ice cream in tiny plastic cups with a wooden lollipop stick poking out. My mum always tells me that when kids came out of school, they would go in search of these women to buy an ice cream every single day; even the adults would flock to them after work. Back then, you could buy an ice cream for around 20p. There was nothing much to the ice cream, just *laban* (the equivalent of buttermilk, but savoury) and a dash of rose flavouring. As the years went by, the women would introduce other flavours, such as Vimto, mango or even chai. The culinary genius behind these treats essentially involved pouring drinks into cups and freezing them, yet despite their simplicity, they were revolutionary for the ice-cream scene in the capital, and remain a nostalgic memory for many Omanis.

In the UK, I find the buttermilk available in supermarkets to be too thin and lacking creaminess, so my version is made with a typical egg yolk-based ice cream. The addition of rambutans brightens the flavour and brings a slight sourness while adding a refreshing touch. If you can't find canned rambutans, you can use canned lychees; the flavour comes out more or less the same.

Blend the rambutans in a blender until smooth, then set aside.

In a bowl, whisk the egg yolks with half the sugar, then set aside.

In a saucepan over a medium heat, slowly heat the cream and rose water with the rest of the sugar until it bubbles around the sides.

Pour a small amount of the warm cream into the eggs, whisking as you add it, to temper. Keep adding the cream, a little at a time, until you've added half, whisking all the while. Now pour the egg-yolk mixture into the pan of cream. Whisk well, then remove from the heat and leave to cool – the buttermilk can't be added to a hot mixture.

Once the cream is cool, add it to the blender with the rambutans. Pour in the buttermilk and blend to combine, then pour into a freezer-proof container and chill in the fridge overnight to mature.

Transfer to the freezer the next day and freeze for 2 hours. Blend once more, then return to the freezer and enjoy once frozen!

Mishmish
Ice Cream

Apricot & Dried Lime
Ice Cream

Serves 5–6

300g (10oz) pitted apricots
50g (¼ cup) + 2 tbsp soft dark
    brown sugar
1 tsp ground cardamom
400ml (1¾ cups) full-fat milk
100ml (6½ tbsp) double
    (heavy) cream
½ vanilla pod
3 cardamom pods
50g (¼ cup) soft light brown sugar
3 dried limes (pierced)
3 egg yolks
1 tsp sea salt flakes

In April, the mountainous terrains of Oman are abundant with succulent yellow apricots. Most of them are sold before they are even harvested. This is true for a lot of our fruit produce, as people from all over the Gulf travel to join our food and produce-related auctions. I was in Oman in April 2021, and I searched high and low for Omani apricots. Locals told me it would be near enough impossible, as most would already be sold, and I'd be better off buying imported Iranian ones from the shop. It took me about a week, a *lot* of perseverance and a 60-km (37-mile) car journey, but I managed to find some in Wakan village, located in the Dakhiliyah Governorate, which has some of the best and most unique climate conditions in the north. Getting hold of those apricots felt like a major victory, and with temperatures in the high thirties (Celsius), nothing seemed more appropriate and celebratory than ice cream. Thus, this *mishmish* ("apricot" in Arabic) ice cream was born – and every spoonful was worth the effort.

Preheat the oven to 190°C (170°C fan/375°F/Gas 5).

In a bowl, combine the apricots with the 2 tablespoons dark brown sugar and the ground cardamom. Mix well to coat the apricots, then tip on to a baking tray and roast for 35 minutes.

Meanwhile, in a saucepan, combine the milk, cream, vanilla, cardamom pods, half the light brown sugar and the dried limes. Place over a low heat and bring to a simmer. Leave this to simmer for at least 10 minutes without bubbling, to allow the dried lime to infuse.

In a separate bowl, whisk together the egg yolks and remaining sugar.

Once you start to see steam and a few bubbles forming around the edges of the cream mixture, remove from the heat and slowly pour it into your egg mixture, whisking all the while so the eggs don't scramble.

Once incorporated, pour the mixture back into the saucepan, still over a low heat, and stir continuously while the custard thickens ever so slightly. This will take just 3–5 minutes; no longer, or it may split. If you have a cooking thermometer, 82°C (180°F) is the perfect temperature. Leave to cool for a little while, then strain through a sieve.

Tip the roasted apricots into a blender and blend (skin on) until you have a smooth purée. Stir this into the custard, along with the salt. Leave to cool completely, then place in the fridge overnight to mature.

The next day, churn in an ice-cream machine according to the manufacturer's instructions. If you don't have an ice-cream machine, you can blend in a blender for 1 minute instead, then freeze for 2 hours, then blend again and freeze until you are ready to eat.

Rangeena

Toasted Flour, Date &
Cherry Tartlets

Serves 8

425g (scant 3½ cups) plain
(all-purpose) flour
40g (scant ¼ cup) caster
(superfine) sugar
120g (1 stick) cold unsalted butter
3 egg yolks
5 tbsp milk (if needed)

For the filling
335g (11¾oz) frozen sour cherries
20g (scant 2 tbsp) caster
(superfine) sugar
½ tsp ground cardamom
zest of 1 lime
4 tbsp orange juice
250g (9oz) Medjool dates, finely
chopped, or date paste

For the crumble
55g (generous ¼ cup) soft light
brown sugar
45g (scant ¼ cup) soft dark brown
sugar
90g (6 tbsp) unsalted butter
150g (5oz) shelled pistachios, very
finely chopped

Rangeena is a traditional date dessert mainly made by people who come from Muscat and have a connection to Bahrain, like my father's family. My Auntie Munira sometimes serves it at her Saturday family lunches. I have adapted it slightly to create these tartlets. Serve hot with vanilla ice cream or custard – delightful.

Preheat the oven to 200°C (180°C fan/400°F/Gas 6) and line a baking tray with baking parchment (parchment paper). Tip the flour into the prepared tray. Spread it out evenly, then toast in the oven for 30 minutes. Remove and leave to cool completely.

The flour's weight will have reduced after toasting. Separate out 230g (1¾ cups) flour for the pastry and keep the rest for the crumble.

Sift the toasted flour for the pastry into a large bowl. Add the sugar and butter, then use your hands to rub the mixture together until it resembles breadcrumbs. Add the egg yolks and continue to work the mixture together. If it won't bind, gradually add the milk. Once you have a smooth dough, bring it together into a ball and wrap in cling film (plastic wrap). Flatten it out slightly and refrigerate for 3–4 hours or overnight.

Meanwhile, for the filling, add the cherries to a small saucepan with the sugar, cardamom, lime zest and orange juice. Place over a high heat and bring to the boil for 10 minutes, then set aside.

For the crumble, combine the reserved toasted flour, both sugars and the butter in a mixing bowl, along with 50g (1¾oz) of the pistachios. Use your fingers to massage everything together.

When you're ready to cook, preheat your oven to 200°C (180°C fan/400°F/Gas 6). Divide the dough into 8 pieces, then roll out each one to about 2mm (⅛in) thick and use them to line 8 mini tart tins. Prick the bases of the dough with a fork, then cover each mini tart case with baking parchment and fill with baking beans or dried rice. Blind-bake the tart cases for 12–13 minutes, then remove the baking parchment and baking beans and bake for a further 5 minutes.

Once the tart cases are ready, remove them from the oven (but leave the oven on). Divide the dates or date paste evenly between the tart cases, packing them tightly, then top each one with about 1 tablespoon (or slightly more) of the cherry mixture, along with some of the juices. Scatter the crumble mixture over the top of each, then bake for 20–25 minutes, to let the crumble brown.

Sprinkle over the remaining pistachios and serve hot, with ice cream or custard.

Sticky Toffee Pudding

Serves 6

45g (3 tbsp) unsalted butter, plus extra for greasing

100g (generous ¾ cup) self-raising flour, plus extra for dusting

100g (3½oz) dates, roughly chopped

250ml (1 cup plus 1 tbsp) milk

1 vanilla pod or ½ tsp vanilla extract

85g (7 tbsp) demerara (Turbinado) sugar

1 egg, beaten

½ tsp bicarbonate of soda (baking soda)

zest and juice of 4 mandarins

25g (scant 1oz) walnuts, roughly chopped

1 tbsp treacle or date molasses

For the caramel sauce

100g (½ cup) golden caster (superfine) sugar

75g (6½ tbsp) soft dark brown sugar

55g (3½ tbsp) unsalted butter, cut into small pieces

1 vanilla pod or ½ tsp vanilla extract

pinch of salt

200ml (scant 1 cup) double (heavy) cream

In Oman, we have a traditional sweet known as *halwa*, which is made with sugar cane and lots of ghee, and flavoured with an array of spices, dried fruits and nuts, such as saffron, cardamom, rose or figs. It's cooked and stirred for four hours in a large copper pan until it turns from liquid to a thick, jelly-like consistency, similar to that of Turkish delight, but slightly looser. Although machines are able to churn it now, Omanis will tell you there is a really big difference in the flavour and texture, so eating traditional, handmade *halwa* is always the best way. While I would love to teach you how to make *halwa*, it's honestly one of those things you must just buy when you visit Oman. I'm also a little wary of offering it to non-Omanis, as it can be quite hit-or-miss – you can only eat a teaspoon at a time due to how sweet it is, and the texture takes some getting used to. But once you're familiar with it, your lunchtime coffee or evening tea will be completely elevated.

While *halwa* is, alas, too difficult to make at home, this sticky toffee pudding echoes its rich flavours in the best possible way. In this recipe, I've also added a shot of acidity with the mandarins; a match made in *halwa* heaven. If you can't find mandarins, clementines will work too.

Preheat the oven to 200°C (180°C fan/400°F/Gas 6). Butter and flour six 200ml (7oz) ramekins and set aside.

Combine the dates with the milk in a saucepan over a medium–high heat. Bring to the boil and boil for about 5 minutes until the dates soften, then set aside to cool. Once cool, I like to use a stick blender to purée this mixture so there aren't any bits, but that is optional.

In a mixing bowl, whisk the butter, vanilla and sugar until pale, then add the egg and beat together.

Sift in the flour and bicarbonate of soda and mix, then add the mandarin zest and juice, followed by the walnuts, treacle or date molasses, and the milk and date mixture. Fold until everything is well combined.

Pour the mixture into the prepared ramekins, filling them about three-quarters full, then bake for 20–25 minutes until firm, and a skewer inserted into the middle comes out clean.

Meanwhile, to make the caramel sauce, combine both sugars in a saucepan, along with the butter, vanilla, salt and half the cream. Place over a medium–high heat and bring to the boil. Stir until everything has melted together and the mixture has turned a deep caramel colour. Remove the sauce from the heat and pour in the rest of the cream, then stir through.

To serve, turn your puddings out of their ramekins on to plates and pour the caramel sauce over the top, then enjoy. These are delicious with cream or ice cream, too.

Karkade

Hibiscus & Rose Drink

Serves 6

60g (2oz) dried hibiscus petals
10g (¼ oz) dried rose petals
80g (6½ tbsp) caster (superfine)
    sugar
ice, to serve

We used to have a restaurant in Muscat called Kargeen. It was *the* hot spot to go to in town, and always a great place to take visitors, as the vibes were very Omani. I developed a habit of going there almost every other day when I was in town. You were always guaranteed great shisha and a huge glass of *karkade* (Arabic for "hibiscus") slushie, which was always so cold, sweet, sour and delicious. I never wanted to make the drink myself; I just wanted to sit there, people-watch and sip away. The restaurant closed down in 2020, and it's definitely missed by the whole city – and now I have no choice but to make my own version of this delicious drink. You could turn it into a slushie by adding lots of crushed ice, but I prefer it this way. If you can't get hold of rose petals, try using a tablespoon of dried lavender instead. You can always make it without if you prefer.

Combine the hibiscus, rose petals and sugar with 2 litres (8½ cups) of water in a large saucepan. Bring to the boil over a high heat, and leave to boil vigorously for 20 minutes.

Take off the heat and leave to cool completely, then strain and refrigerate until chilled.

Serve over ice. This will keep in the fridge for up to a week.

Limon Nana

Mint Lemonade

Serves 4

25g (scant 1oz) fresh mint leaves
60g (generous ¼ cup) caster
    (superfine) sugar
110ml (scant ½ cup) freshly
    squeezed lemon juice
600ml (2½ cups) sparkling water
    (or still, if you prefer)
ice, to serve

This is probably the most famous drink to come out of the Middle East. Even though I can make it in the UK, it just seems to hit differently when you have it there. A perfect summertime refresher.

Combine the mint, sugar, lemon juice and water in a blender with a few ice cubes and blend until smooth.

Strain, then serve over ice. This will keep in the fridge for 2–3 days.

Omani Chai

Cardamom Za'atar Tea

Serves 2

170g (scant 6oz) evaporated milk
4 cardamom pods, crushed
1 tsp dried za'atar leaves or
　dried thyme
2 black tea bags

I am not a tea drinker at all, but my mother always has a cuppa in her hand; she drinks it like it's going out of fashion. While I don't drink tea, it turns out that I am, somehow, great at making it. In Oman, each family's version of this tea differs depending on their *qabeela* (see page 22) and influences.

　Cardamom has always been the way Bibi has done it, as that is common in Zanzibar, while my mum switches between cardamom, saffron, cloves and za'atar. For this recipe, you need dried za'atar leaves, which you can source online or in Middle Eastern countries, as opposed to the za'atar herb blend sold in some supermarkets. If you can't get it, dried thyme works just as well. You'll have to rely on my family's taste buds for this, as I tested many versions on them and this was their favourite combination. It makes two perfect mugs, so I hope you and whoever you choose to share it with enjoy it.

Add all the ingredients to a saucepan with 450ml (scant 2 cups) of water and bring to the boil over a medium–high heat.

Boil for exactly 7 minutes, then let it settle for a minute before serving.

Strain into two mugs and enjoy.

Laban

Mint & Cumin Yogurt Drink

Serves 4

500g (2 cups) full-fat yogurt
½ tsp salt, or to taste
15g (½oz) mint leaves
1 tsp cumin seeds
ice cubes

Laban, also known as *ayran* in Turkey and *doogh* in Iran, is a popular savoury yogurt drink. This is an everyday beverage in Oman, but is particularly popular during Ramadan. Although we say "yogurt", the way it's served in Oman is more similar to buttermilk, as the milk is left to ferment and then churned to remove the butter. If you ever get to go to Oman, please do try to find it fresh – there is nothing quite like it! I've used yogurt in my version, as I find it gives it a better consistency than supermarket buttermilk. You can find *laban* in an array of flavours; this cumin and mint recipe is inspired by my road trips around Oman.

Combine the yogurt, salt, mint leaves and cumin seeds in a blender with 500ml (generous 2 cups) of water and a few cubes of ice. Blitz until smooth.

Chill in the fridge for at least an hour, then serve over ice; if you like, you can strain it as you pour to remove any bits. This will keep in the fridge for up to a week.

INTERIOR

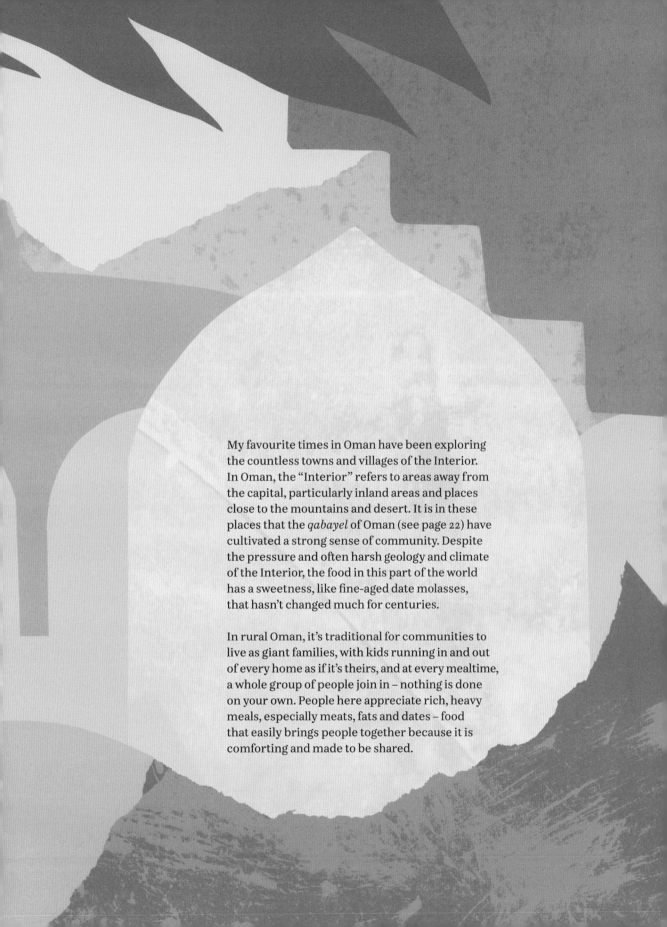

My favourite times in Oman have been exploring the countless towns and villages of the Interior. In Oman, the "Interior" refers to areas away from the capital, particularly inland areas and places close to the mountains and desert. It is in these places that the *qabayel* of Oman (see page 22) have cultivated a strong sense of community. Despite the pressure and often harsh geology and climate of the Interior, the food in this part of the world has a sweetness, like fine-aged date molasses, that hasn't changed much for centuries.

In rural Oman, it's traditional for communities to live as giant families, with kids running in and out of every home as if it's theirs, and at every mealtime, a whole group of people join in – nothing is done on your own. People here appreciate rich, heavy meals, especially meats, fats and dates – food that easily brings people together because it is comforting and made to be shared.

Madhrouba

Dried Lime Chicken & Rice Balls with Coriander Aioli

Makes 15

120g (generous ½ cup) white
    basmati rice
3 tbsp vegetable oil, plus
    500ml (generous 2 cups)
    for deep-frying
1 onion, finely chopped
2 tbsp garlic paste
2 tsp ground cumin
1 tsp ground turmeric
2 tsp ground coriander
1 tsp ground black pepper
2 fresh tomatoes, finely diced
3 dried limes
600g (1lb 5oz) boneless,
    skinless chicken thighs (about
    6–7 pieces)
salt, to taste
small handful of sage leaves
    (about 16 leaves), finely
    chopped

For coating the balls
2 large eggs
100g (generous ¾ cup) plain
    (all-purpose) flour
150g (5½oz) breadcrumbs

For the aioli
1 large egg
200ml (scant 1 cup) extra virgin
    olive oil
1 garlic clove, crushed or finely
    chopped
50g (1¾oz) coriander (cilantro),
    finely chopped
sea salt flakes, to taste
juice of 1 lime

Madhrouba literally translates from Arabic as "beaten rice". This dish is mainly made by Omanis with Bahraini ancestry and Bahrainis, but it's sometimes seen in other Gulf countries and among the Bedouin community. Traditionally, it's served as a rice porridge, made with chicken, fresh tuna or lamb, but you could use crab, or even melt-in-the-mouth goat meat, if you like. Here, I've shaped the *madhrouba* into balls, almost like arancini, inspired by my good friend Abdullah, who had the idea when we worked together on a menu for a kitchen takeover at a hotel in the south of Oman. Of course, you can keep the *madhrouba* in its original porridge-like form if you prefer – it's a great comforting dish for the winter. You can opt for any part of the chicken for this recipe, and if you use on-the-bone chicken, you will yield an even better flavour, but then it's a case of picking out the bones. The aioli is a non-traditional addition that I've created for supper clubs; if you are entertaining guests, it's a perfect choice.

Rinse the rice well under running water, then tip into a bowl. Pour over enough water to cover and leave to soak for at least 20 minutes or while the chicken is cooking.

Heat the 3 tablespoons of oil in a large saucepan over a high heat. Add the onion and fry for around 10 minutes until beginning to brown. Stir in the garlic, along with the spices and tomatoes, and fry for 2 minutes more.

Break the shells of the dried limes and remove the inside skin, discarding the seeds. Roughly tear the dried lime skins then add to the saucepan, along with the chicken pieces and 1 litre (4⅓ cups) of water. Season with salt, then cover with a lid and leave to boil for 45 minutes on a medium–high heat until the chicken is cooked through and very tender. Reduce the heat to low and, one piece at a time, remove the chicken pieces and shred into long, thin strands using two forks – the meat should fall apart. Once shredded, return the chicken to the saucepan.

Drain the rice and add it to the saucepan. Stir well, then add 500ml (generous 2 cups) of water. Increase the heat to medium, then cover and leave to cook for 15 minutes. Remove the lid and stir, then add the sage leaves and leave to simmer, uncovered, for another 25–30 minutes, stirring every 5 minutes to stop it from sticking. You want the water to be fully absorbed, the rice to have broken down and the mixture to have come together like a thick porridge.

Recipe continues overleaf

Remove from the heat and leave to cool completely, then place in the fridge for at least 15–20 minutes to chill and become firmer – this will make it easier to shape it into balls.

Meanwhile, make the aioli. In a bowl, combine the egg, half the oil, the garlic and the coriander. Season with salt to taste, then blend with a hand-held blender until the mixture emulsifies and thickens. Add the remaining oil and lime juice, and continue to blend until combined. Place in a jar and leave to chill in the fridge until needed. (If you don't have a blender, you can do this by hand, but it will take longer and you will need to add the oil gradually.)

When you're ready to cook, use clean hands to shape the rice mixture into 15 balls, each one slightly bigger than a golf ball.

To coat the balls, whisk the eggs in a bowl, then scatter the flour and the breadcrumbs on to separate plates.

Roll each ball in the flour, then the eggs, then the breadcrumbs, making sure each one is well coated.

Heat the oil for shallow-frying in a large frying pan over a high heat. The oil should be deep enough to come about a quarter of the way up the balls when you add them. To check if the oil is hot enough, add the first ball – it should begin to sizzle straight away. If so, add the remaining balls and fry for 2–3 minutes on each side until they are a deep golden colour. Once they are cooked, transfer to a plate lined with kitchen paper (paper towels) to soak up the excess oil.

Serve hot with the aioli for dipping.

Masanaf

Split Pea & Okra Pancakes

Makes about 8

For the filling

50g (1¾oz) split peas

4 tbsp vegetable or olive oil, plus
    extra for shallow-frying
    (optional)

200g (7oz) okra, finely chopped

½ red onion, finely chopped

1 tbsp coriander seeds, ground

1 tbsp cumin seeds, ground

1 tsp freshly ground black pepper

1 tbsp garlic paste

15g (½oz) parsley, finely chopped

1 green chilli, finely chopped
    (optional)

salt, to taste

For the batter

200g (generous 1½ cups) flour

1 egg

pinch of salt

Cooking notes:

I prefer to use whole coriander
seeds and cumin seeds and grind
them myself, as this gives a stronger
flavour, but you can use ground
coriander and cumin if you prefer.

When pouring the batter into the
frying pan, I like to use a mould or
cookie cutter about 8cm (3in) in
diameter so I can get these perfectly
round, but it's not a must.

The last step involves shallow-
frying, for an extra golden touch
and crunch, but you can miss it
out if you prefer.

This recipe is made in both Oman and Zanzibar. *Masanaf* are usually
filled with meat, but there are two ways of making the dough exterior.
In Oman, it is mainly made like pizza dough, but you keep on rolling it
with ghee until it is super thin, then wrap it around the filling meat.
I prefer it my grandmother's way: making a pancake-like batter and
then cooking and filling it. It's a lot simpler and quicker! You can fill
these with whatever you like, using the same spice mixture, but I find
okra and split peas create the perfect combination of flavour and
texture. Please note that the peas require overnight soaking.

Place the split peas in a bowl and pour over boiling water to cover.
Leave to soak overnight.

The next day, drain the split peas, then transfer to a saucepan.
Fill the pan with fresh water and bring to the boil over a high heat.
Boil for 45–60 minutes until the split peas are soft.

Heat 3 tablespoons of the oil in a frying pan over a high heat. Add the
okra and sauté for about 5 minutes until no longer sticky/slimy. Add
the onion, spices, garlic paste and parsley, along with the chilli, if using,
and fry for a further 2–3 minutes, then stir in the split peas. Season with
salt to taste and set aside.

Make the batter by whisking the flour, egg and salt in a bowl with 160ml
(generous ⅔ cup) of water.

To make the pancakes, heat a frying pan over a high heat and brush it
with 1 tablespoon of the oil.

Pour some of the batter into the pan; it should be about 8cm (3in) in
diameter. Quickly add around 1 heaped tablespoon of the filling into
the middle, then pour or spoon more batter on top to cover the filling.

Cook for 2–3 minutes until the bottom is cooked, then flip the pancake
over and cook for 2–3 minutes on the other side. Transfer to a plate, then
repeat until all the batter and filling have been used up.

Once all the pancakes are made, you have the option of shallow-frying
them to crisp them up and add more colour. If you wish to do this, pour
some more oil into the pan; it should be deep enough to come about
halfway up the pancakes. Return the pancakes to the pan, working in
batches, and shallow-fry them for 2–3 minutes on each side until
crunchy and golden.

Serve as a snack or side dish. I enjoy these with chilli sauce and my
homemade Tamarind Sauce (see page 181)!

Interior

Bibi Mosa's Qeliah/Tqeliah

Grape Vinegar Stewed Lamb

Serves 2–3

500g (1lb 2oz) lamb shoulder
    (or another cut if you prefer),
    chopped into 2.5cm (1in) pieces
    (no bones; little or no fat)
1 tbsp garlic paste
120ml (½ cup) grape vinegar
1 tsp salt
2 tsp black peppercorns
1 tbsp coriander seeds
1 tbsp cumin seeds
1 red onion, thinly sliced
flatbread, chapati or paratha,
    to serve
fresh coriander (cilantro) leaves
    (optional), to serve
honey, to serve

In the 400-year-old *wilayat* (province) of Al Hamra, located in the north-east of Oman, lives Mosa, the grandmother of my friend Zahra and the cutest and sassiest grandma there is, Bibi Mosa. She always feeds me until I can't breathe, and then tells me to wear a scarf so I look "like a bride".

Despite this, visiting Bibi Mosa is a tranquil experience. Al Hamra is home to the ancient village of Misfat Al Arabiyeen, a serene mountain oasis known for its self-sustaining *falaj* irrigation system. Some of the best honey in the country is produced on this mountain, with people from all over the Gulf travelling there in season to buy litres of every type on offer: *sidr, sumar* and *zah'r*.

Qeliah (sometimes known as *tqeliah*, depending on where you are from) is a celebration dish eaten in this area during Eid. The meat is traditionally stewed in date vinegar until very tender, and when serving, they pour over local honey and scoop it up with paper-thin Omani bread. I have kept this recipe as close to Bibi Mosa's as possible, with a few alterations – for example, I've used grape vinegar instead of the traditional date version as it's easier to source in the UK. Fig or another berry vinegar would also work, as long as it's not balsamic. The honey is 100 per cent essential; it really balances the dish.

In a large saucepan, combine the lamb, garlic, vinegar and salt with 400ml (1¾ cups) of water. Place over a medium heat and leave to cook, uncovered, for 30 minutes.

Grind the peppercorns, coriander seeds and cumin seeds using a pestle and mortar, then add to the pan, along with the onion. Cover and leave to simmer for another hour until the lamb is tender and the sauce has reduced and thickened.

Serve with flatbread, chapati or paratha, and a scattering of coriander leaves, if you like. Drizzle honey over your plate before eating, or scoop up the meat with the bread and dip in honey.

BEDOUINS OF OMAN

Meeting Najah and her family in their haven was the first time I truly witnessed the meaning of a matriarchy. Deep in the desert, surrounded by nothing but roaming goats, date palm huts and loyal camels, I spent time with women who had the poise to lead a whole village. My friend Najah is from a nomadic desert family known as Bedouins. For centuries, they have travelled through the desert to the coast with their camels and goats. During the 1970s, when the late Sultan Qaboos came into power, he focused on the Bedouins in his bid to unite the country and its people, and tried to encourage them to move into the villages and cities to provide them with education and jobs. At the time, this was resisted by Bedouins, but over the years, as the country transformed, they began to see the benefits. Bedouins integrated into the wider communities by being paired up with families who lived close to the desert. They spent time in these families' homes while they took a break from their travels, allowing them to ease into the different lifestyle.

Today, Bedouins live both lifestyles happily; the younger generation are more inclined to be with the wider society, while their parents hold on to tradition and carry on spending time in the desert. Najah, along with her mother and aunties, still visits the desert every weekend or during holidays. They took me to visit their area, which is slightly outside a city called Manah, and it was such an interesting experience. All the women wear a *batoola*, a traditional Bedouin mask. Some of the older women sleep in their *batoola* – it is such a special and beloved part of their culture. The women collected my cousin and I in their pick-up trucks, which was the first time I had ever seen a woman drive such a vehicle in Oman. Paired with their traditional dress and masks, it was a sight I will never forget.

On our way to the desert, I noticed husbands and children weren't joining us. According to Najah, this was a chance for the women to get away, to leave their husbands with the kids and enjoy their time from sunset to sunrise to talk about their days, share poems, eat, pray and enjoy one another's company.

When we reached the desert, the older women knew exactly where to go. Without hesitation, they took us to their fabric tent. To me, it looked like every single one we had passed on the drive, but they guided us to the exact spot by following the sunset and searching for specific plants. The intuition of these women was astonishing. To confirm their spot, one of the aunties rummaged in a plant and pulled out a teacup. She told me this is how they know the space belongs to them; after their last cup of tea before leaving in the morning, they place the cup upside down in a plant, and that lets them identify their spot and stop other Bedouins from taking over their space. They do this in various locations, to always have a home wherever they travel.

We arrived just in time for sunset prayers. All the women removed their masks, and we prayed side by side. Seeing them barefaced was surreal; the masks created such an armour that the women appeared invincible, but when they were removed, I had the pleasure of witnessing the most beautiful Omani women I had ever seen.

That night, we cooked flatbread on hot coals and made *aish wa haleeb* with dried goat meat coated in cinnamon and chilli (see page 84 for my version). The rice was cooked for a long time and topped off with goat's milk to create a soft texture, almost like risotto. Najah served it on a large platter, and we huddled on the ground eating the rice as the aunties told us stories of their travels and the things they'd learned in the desert.

Interior

Aish wa Haleeb

Milky Goat & Cinnamon Risotto

Serves 6

500g (1lb 2oz) goat, cut into 2.5cm (1in) pieces, ideally with a couple of bones
2 tbsp + 2 tsp ground cinnamon
1½ tsp chilli powder
2 tsp ground turmeric
1 tbsp garlic paste
3 tbsp olive oil
2 tsp salt
2 red onions, 1 cut into 8 wedges and 1 finely chopped
200g (1 cup) risotto rice
2 carrots, shredded or chopped
2 celery sticks, chopped (optional)
4 bay leaves
1 tbsp fenugreek seeds
400ml (1¾ cups) full-fat goat's milk

The first time I made this dish, I did it with basmati rice. You can still use that if you prefer, but I feel risotto rice gives the best texture. The addition of carrots was very much me; the dish is very rich, so adding any vegetable you enjoy, particularly something with a crunchy texture, will help. This also works with lamb if you can't source goat – lamb will take less time to cook. I use Ceylon cinnamon in this; it is sweeter and has a lighter colour. We usually serve this with a leafy, lemony salad and also *laban* (also known as *ayran*, a salty yogurt drink – see page 70), pouring little amounts over as we eat.

In a bowl, combine the meat with 2 tablespoons of the cinnamon, along with the chilli powder, turmeric, garlic paste, olive oil and salt. Mix to combine. If possible, leave to marinate for at least 1 hour.

In a large saucepan, combine the marinated goat meat with the red onion wedges and 1 litre (4⅓ cups) of water (there should be enough water to cover the meat). Cover and place over a medium–high heat. Leave to boil for 1½–2 hours until the meat is soft and cooked through.

Once the meat is ready, the liquid will have reduced, so add another 400ml (1¾ cups) of water, along with the rice, finely chopped onion, carrots, celery (if using), bay leaves, fenugreek seeds and the rest of the cinnamon. The water should just cover the rice and meat, but not by too much. Taste for seasoning and add some more salt if needed.

Bring to the boil, then securely wrap a clean tea towel round your saucepan lid and put it on top of the pan to lock in the steam. Reduce to the lowest heat and steam for 30 minutes.

Stir in the goat's milk, then cover with the lid once more. Cook for another 30 minutes, still on a low heat, until the rice has absorbed the milk.

Serve with your chosen accompaniments.

Khoubz Bedou

Bedouin Bread/
Goat's Milk Flatbread

Makes 10

1kg (scant 8 cups) "00" fine flour,
    plus extra for dusting
750ml (3 cups) goat's milk
7g (scant ¼ oz) fast-action
    dried yeast (1 packet)
50ml (scant ¼ cup) olive oil,
    plus extra for brushing
1 tbsp salt

This bread is basically *tanoor* bread, *tanoor* meaning "firepit". I've called it Bedouin bread because whenever I go to visit the Bedouins in the desert, they always make it. A man will sit there kneading huge amounts of dough on the ground until it is super soft, then he will roll it out into big pieces and cook them over the fire pit. Eating this bread directly after it's come off the flames is my favourite thing; it's so warm and soft. I started making this for a menu I was working on at a hotel in Abu Dhabi, and it received so many compliments. I love how something so simple makes so many people happy. The beauty of using goat's milk is it helps to keep the bread soft, but also brings a slight tang to it.

In this recipe, I use "00" fine flour. This is a habit I picked up at the hotel, as it gives the dough the softest touch, but you can also use plain (all-purpose) flour if you wish.

Add all the ingredients to a mixer fitted with a dough hook and knead for 15–20 minutes until the dough is very smooth and elasticated.

Cover with a clean cloth and leave to rise for 1 hour until doubled in size.

Knock back the dough and divide it into 10 pieces. On a lightly floured surface, roll each one into a circle about 30cm (12in) in diameter, making sure it's no more than 5mm (¼in) thick. You can make smaller breads if you prefer, just make sure to keep to the same thickness.

Preheat a barbecue or place a griddle pan over a high heat. Brush the barbecue rack or griddle pan with olive oil to stop the bread from sticking, and once it's super hot, place the first flatbread on the rack or griddle pan. As it cooks, it will begin to bubble on top. Cook for 2–3 minutes until slightly brown on the bottom. Flip and cook the other side for 1–2 minutes.

Repeat with the remaining breads and serve. These are best eaten warm on the day they're made, but will keep for up to a day wrapped in cling film (plastic wrap) at room temperature.

Shuwa

48-hour Spiced Lamb

Serves 6–8

2 tbsp black peppercorns

1 tbsp coriander seeds

1 cinnamon stick

5 cloves

1 tbsp cumin seeds

5 cardamom pods

1 tsp ground nutmeg

2 tbsp chilli flakes

100ml (scant ½ cup) red wine vinegar

2 dried limes, ground to a fine powder

1 tbsp salt

10 garlic cloves, crushed, or 3 tbsp garlic paste

50ml (scant ¼ cup) vegetable oil

1 leg of lamb or 1 sheep shoulder, about 1.5–2kg (3lb 3oz–4½lb)

Whenever someone tells you they've tried Omani food, 99 per cent of the time, they've had *shuwa*. *Shuwa* is recognised as our national dish, despite only being made in the northern half of the country. We pride ourselves on this dish, and it is loved across the Gulf. It showcases a slow-roasted lamb, sheep, goat or sometimes camel, which is bathed for up to 48 hours in a spice blend. No two *shuwa* recipes are ever the same, as each spice blend pays homage to that family's heritage. Trying to get someone to share their recipe with me was so difficult; every person wants to take it to their grave. In our family, my father's brother, Uncle Habib, was known for making the best *shuwa*; my mum still remembers eating it when she lived in Oman. The only person who knew the recipe was his driver, who helped him prepare kilos of marinade ahead of Eid so that all his siblings and cousins could send their meat to him for marination. Uncle Habib's son, my cousin Yassir, finally shared the recipe with me after his passing. He knew I could keep the tradition going and I am so glad he trusted me with it. Uncle Habib's recipe is perfect. He's probably turning in his grave knowing that I am sharing it with the world, but it's something you all need to have in your home for a special occasion.

Traditionally, once marinated, the meat is wrapped in banana leaves, popped into a date palm sack and then placed into a deep fire pit in the ground, known as a *tanoor*, on the first day of Eid. It is then removed and eaten on the second or third day. A whole village will share one *tanoor*, yet every person seems to know which sack is theirs. Most families will prepare two sacks: one for themselves and one to pass to the community and any families who are in need.

The slow-cooking of the meat encases it in a thick, decadent crust of spices, leaving the tenderest of flesh that falls straight off the bone, while the date palm sack gives the dish a strong, smoky flavour that is near enough impossible to recreate. Although we could have this at any time of year, we wait eagerly for Eid to practise the whole ritual with family and friends. I have always been determined to hold on to this tradition when I can't be in Oman for Eid, and over the years, my mum and I have managed to get the oven to do it justice. If we are cooking this in the summertime, we tend to finish it on a barbecue to replicate the smokiness. It's best served with saffron or spiced rice, and a yogurt-based salad. The leftovers can be kept until the next day, then fried and tucked inside a warm pitta for a mini shuwarma. This dish takes 12–48 hours to marinate, and about 5 hours to cook.

Recipe continues overleaf

Line a large roasting tray with foil, leaving plenty of foil overhanging as you'll use it to wrap the meat later.

Combine all the spices in a dry frying pan and toast over a medium–high heat for 5 minutes, just until the mixture begins to smoke and you can smell a strong aroma. Ensure you keep stirring the spices as you toast them, and do not leave them on the heat for too long, as they can burn easily and you'll be left with a bitter taste.

Transfer the mixture to a blender or spice grinder and blitz until you have a fine powder.

Tip the ground spice mixture into a pestle and mortar. Add the vinegar, dried lime powder, salt, garlic and oil and mix together to form a paste.

Place your meat on the prepared roasting tray and use a sharp knife to cut small slits all over the meat. This will allow the marinade to get inside.

Pour the marinade over the meat and use your hands to massage it into all the creases, folds and cuts of the meat. Don't worry if you seem to have excess marinade; just pour it all over.

Pull up the overhanging foil and wrap it over the meat so it is sealed like a parcel. Make sure there are NO gaps! We don't want any juice or air to escape during the cooking process.

Leave to marinate in the fridge for at least 12 hours, and up to 48 hours. (If you like, you can even marinate it and then freeze it until you need it.)

When you're ready to cook, take the meat out of the fridge and allow it to reach room temperature. Meanwhile, preheat the oven to 160°C (140°C fan/325°F/Gas 3).

Cook for about 5 hours, until the lamb is tender and falling off the bone. Remove from the oven and leave the meat to rest for around 15 minutes before plating. There will be excess juices in the tray, which you should pour over the top of the lamb to serve.

Harees/Arsiya

Spiced Barley & Chicken Porridge

Serves 4–5

500g (1lb 2oz) chicken legs and
   thighs
150g (5½oz) chicken breast
6 cardamom pods
5 cloves
1 cinnamon stick
2 tsp freshly ground black pepper
1 tsp salt
1 tbsp garlic paste
1 tbsp ginger paste
300g (10oz) pearl barley, soaked
   in water for at least 1 hour
100g (3½oz) ghee
butter, to serve

This is our "ugly-delicious" dish – the best comparison to this would be congee, a rice or barley savoury porridge. *Harees* is the name given when we use pearl barley; it is also made this way in Zanzibar, where it's called *boko boko*. *Arsiya* is the name used when we cook the dish with rice. Both versions can be cooked with chicken or lamb; here, I've used chicken. I grew up with this dish being a once-in-a-while, comforting, curl-up-on-the-sofa-on-a-cold-day type of meal. We eat it more during Ramadan, but in Oman, most families serve this on the first day of Eid. I always really enjoy seeing everyone dressed up, dripping in gold, and then sitting at the table to eat porridge; it has always seemed such a juxtaposition. In Zanzibar, we eat it with *torsha*, a sauce made with dates and tamarind, with the option of liver or lamb (see my recipe on page 93), but my bibi dislikes *torsha*, and sprinkles sugar over hers instead. Whichever you prefer, never forget to add a dollop of butter to your plate and allow it to melt in before you eat.

Place all the chicken in a deep saucepan or casserole pot, along with the spices, salt, and garlic and ginger paste. Pour in 1 litre (4⅓ cups) of water. Rinse and drain the pearl barley, then add this to the pan too. Cover with a lid and bring to the boil over a high heat.

Once bubbling, reduce the heat to low–medium and pour in another 500ml (generous 2 cups) of water. Cover and leave to slowly cook for an hour, checking on it regularly and stirring from time to time to make sure it doesn't stick to the bottom.

After an hour, add another 500ml (generous 2 cups) of water and stir well. The chicken should be coming away from the bone and beginning to break up. Cover once more and leave to cook for another 45 minutes. By this time, the meat will have broken down further. Pick out all the bones and discard, then add the ghee and stir very well. Add another 200ml (scant 1 cup) of water and leave to cook for a further hour until the water is absorbed.

By the end, you should be left with a thick, porridge-like mixture. You can either leave the barley whole, or blend with a hand-held blender until you have a smooth consistency with strands of chicken running through.

Divide between 4–5 bowls. Add a dollop of butter to each portion and allow it to melt over, then serve with *torsha* or sugar.

Torsha

Date & Tamarind Liver

Serves 4–5

50g (1¾oz) tamarind block
50g (1¾oz) sultanas
    (golden raisins)
40g (1½oz) raisins
4 tbsp neutral oil, such as light
    vegetable oil
1 small onion, diced
1 tsp garlic paste
1 tsp ginger paste
250g (9oz) chicken liver, cut into
    small pieces
1 tbsp baharat spice blend (see
    page 120)
½ tbsp ground cinnamon
50ml (scant ¼ cup)
    red wine vinegar
50g (1¾oz) date molasses
1 tsp salt

Torsha is a sweet, sour liver sauce. In Zanzibar, we eat it with a barley porridge called *harees* or *arsiya* (see page 91 for my version, also pictured here). In Oman, however, *torsha* is only served with *harees* cooked with rice, not barley. I actually prefer eating it served over plain rice, like you would a curry, which my mum thinks is blasphemy! Traditionally, *torsha* is made with liver and lamb, but my mum and I prefer it with just the liver. I have never really been fond of liver and its texture, but there is something about this recipe that I love.

Before you begin, soak the tamarind in 170ml (scant ¾ cup) of water for a couple of hours or overnight.

When you're ready to start cooking, combine the sultanas and raisins in a bowl and pour over 350ml (1½ cups) of water. Leave to soak while you're cooking.

Heat the oil in a large saucepan over a high heat. Add the onion and sweat for 5–6 minutes, then add the garlic and ginger pastes and sauté for another minute.

Add the liver and fry for a further 6–7 minutes, stirring often, adding slightly more oil if the onion and liver start to stick to the pan.

After soaking, your tamarind should have softened into a pulp. Strain the pulp through a sieve to remove the seeds, then add the tamarind pulp and soaking water to the pan. Stir in the remaining ingredients, along with the sultanas and raisins, and 3 tablespoons of their soaking water.

Leave the *torsha* to simmer over a low-medium heat for 20 minutes, until the liver is cooked through and the sauce has become slightly thicker, then serve.

Cooking note:

If you prefer your liver a little pink, you can fry the liver pieces for 2 minutes on each side in a separate pan, then add them to the sauce and cook for a further 2 minutes.

THE SOUTH
OF OMAN

Salalah is my favourite place in Oman. I always say that I'll retire to a villa there, on the white, sandy beaches shaded from the blazing sun by coconut palms. The region, Dhofar, is said to have been settled as early as the 12th century BCE. Today, it is truly majestic, with tropical climates, precious golden frankincense, cascading aqua waterfalls, and emerald-green landscapes weaving into rugged, sky-piercing mountains.

When I was working on my proposal for *Bahari*, I went to stay with some friends in Salalah – Talal and Fatin. I didn't know much about what dishes really came from Salalah or the Dhofar region; as a matter of fact, most people from the north of Oman don't know, either. There is something of a stereotype that Dhofaris like to overindulge in camel meat and grilling over hot stones, known as *mathbi*, but little is known of the array of other dishes they make. Foraging from the sea and mountains is a way of life for Dhofaris; after monsoon season, the women will walk the full length of the beaches in search of tiny clams known as *fithik*, which they boil lightly with spices and onions. The spring months are the most treasured thanks to the beefy blush-red lobsters that are caught from spear-fishing, as well as the rare, iridescent-shelled abalone; these are a real delicacy, as they are only in season for one month in the year, and sell for up to 125 Omani rials (£250) a kilo!

As you travel further inland, you are met with mountains full of farmers herding their cattle, camels and goats. Traditionally, the Dhofaris have always been herders, especially the Jebalis (people who originated from the mountains, *jebel* meaning "mountain" in Arabic). They were among the first people to domesticate animals, in particular cattle and sheep. Both fresh and dried meat are eaten on this side of Dhofar, prepared using methods that have been practised for hundreds of years. Blazing hot rocks are used to grill meat but also to warm milk, bringing a pleasantly smoky touch to it.

Most of all, whether cooking from the land or the sea, the people are ruled by ghee, which is prevalent in all their cooking. I have never tasted ghee so sweet and addictive, and in Dhofar they pour it over everything. Ghee is so important in their culture that it is traditional for a bride-to-be to eat ghee for 40 days before her wedding to help her gain weight, as she is seen as more desirable to her husband with a plumper figure.

When I found out that my friend Talal's stepmother, Fatima, lived next door to him, I was over the moon, as many of Oman's recipes rely on the older generation to pass them on verbally. When she found out I loved cooking, she insisted on pulling out all the stops for me, and even slaughtered a whole cow to show her affection and excitement. Auntie Fatima was born in a cave, which was how people from the region had lived for thousands of years. She told me that she didn't leave the mountains until the 1970s, when Sultan Qaboos came into power and united and developed the region. Her story is very much like that of many people from Dhofar of that era; she spoke about how she had never seen an oven or even shampoo! They were very much self-sufficient and relied on what they could find in the mountains to help them live. Their bathing products were made from plants, and food was only cooked over fire. Despite us not understanding each other when speaking, Auntie Fatima and I connected over her *ma'ajeen* recipe (which I have shared on page 98).

Dhofar is an integral part of southern Oman, but its environment, culture and food are worlds apart from its northern counterpart, Muscat. Dhofar is 1,000km (620 miles) away from the capital, and separated by a large desert that, for centuries, isolated Dhofaris from the rest of the country. Before and during the Pan-Arabism movement in the early 1960s, Dhofaris mostly interacted with merchants that travelled via the *bahari* (ocean) from Zanzibar to Muscat. Culturally and socially, they were actually more connected to Yemen, with which they share a border in the south.

The Sultan at the time, Sultan Said bin Taimur, was deeply suspicious of external powers and had sealed the country off from the rest of the modern world in a bid to protect his sultanate from what he believed were destructive forces. During his reign, Omanis were not allowed to work, leave their villages or even buy a car without his express permission. The people of Dhofar, by virtue of their geographical distance from the capital of Muscat, were struggling economically, in a pretty serious way due to extremely tough regulation. Even the timings of when they could visit markets were regulated, affecting how they would cook and eat. There was extreme poverty and famine, and those most deeply affected became prone to the influences of the Arab Nationalist Movement at the time that was sweeping the Arab world. This eventually led to the establishment of a separatist movement, the Dhofar Liberation Front (DLF), with both men and women seeking to incite a rebellion against the Sultan.

By 1970, the Dhofari separatists had engaged with the government forces for quite some time. The key turning point was when the late Sultan Qaboos, Sultan Said's only son, ascended to the throne on 23 July of the same year. Sultan Qaboos continued to engage with the separatists, but in his wisdom, always supported a diplomatic end to the conflict. This culminated in the successful "Arms for Rations" amnesty campaign that saw rebel forces exchange their arms for much needed food, rations and basic necessities and, most importantly, amnesty. The campaign was supported and enforced by the British Royal Air Force. Ultimately this is what the conflict was about: a lack of access to opportunity and resources. Sultan Qaboos reigned for another 50 years, ushering in modern Oman's renaissance. Suddenly, Oman was united, north and south, east and west, and moved out of its self-cast shadow and into the light of the 20th century.

I have been fortunate enough to spend time with three Dhofari women: Auntie Fatima, Auntie Jamila and Sumaya. They opened their homes to me, taught me their recipes and spoke so eloquently of their region's history. Watching these women dressed in extravagant *thobs* (traditional Dhofari dresses), with detailed henna up to their elbows, drenched in gold while they huddled over a blazing flame with a silver saucepan to check on their dishes, I couldn't help but be in awe of their resilience. All of them remember 1970 and the crossover to a new life that came with the arrival of a "new Oman", which they resisted at first.

Since the 12th century, Dhofar has been connected with ancient civilisations, such as the Greeks, Egyptians, Assyrians, Romans and Persians. The region is the world's most important source of frankincense, and played a major role in the so-called "golden age" of trade. Tradesmen from as far afield as China came to seek out these nuggets of aromatic butter-coloured resin. Legend has it that the Queen of Sheba brought frankincense oil to King Solomon from Salalah. Some scholars even suggest Dhofar is Ophir from the Bible. The governorate is home to the tomb of Prophet Hud (or Hood), believed to be a direct descendant of Prophet Noah (as in Noah's Ark), and some of the Middle East's oldest religious inscriptions. Despite their deep-rooted history, Dhofaris came to accept that progressing with the rest of the country would pave the way to a better future for their families. Each of the women I met had a different depiction to share with me: one was born in a cave, and had to adapt to new societal norms and expectations; one was a descendant of East Africa; and one was born into modern Oman, and experienced the pressures of being the first daughter in her family to receive an education and work.

As well as teaching me about food, these three formidable women showed me that Oman's biggest asset is its people. The way they have held onto traditions that have survived war and other struggles, and speak so fondly of their history and country while also moving with the times, is something I will always admire.

Ma'ajeen

Dhofari Beef in a Sweet
Milk Stew

Serves 2

2 tbsp ghee, plus extra to serve
1 small onion, finely diced
300g (10oz) beef sirloin steak,
    cut into thin strips
1 tsp garlic paste
1 tsp ginger paste
330ml (1⅓ cups) double (heavy)
    cream, at room temperature
1 tsp ground cumin
1 tsp ground cinnamon
1 tsp ground turmeric
1 tsp freshly ground black pepper
1 tbsp caster (superfine) sugar
2 tsp salt
60g (2oz) fresh spinach leaves

Ma'ajeen is a typical Jebali dish. It is made with strips or cubes of dried beef, or sometimes camel, that are dried outside over one or two nights during the drier winter months. The fat of the meat is then rendered down and poured all over it, and when this dries, it looks like cloudy cotton around the beef. Traditionally, this is done before Eid, during the holy sacrificing of animals, and meat is dried and preserved to last the whole year. While Omanis in the north have *shuwa* for Eid (see page 88 for my recipe), Auntie Fatima (see page 96) taught me how Dhofaris prepare *ma'ajeen* for the first day of the celebrations.

The meat is heated to melt the fat and slightly soften it, but it still retains its chew. A separate broth is cooked using fresh cow's milk from the mountains; it's so pure and fresh, our stomachs would probably struggle! This is spiced and sweetened with sugar before being served with rice and fresh, sweet ghee. When eating the dish, everything is served separately, and you layer each element and scoop it up with your hands, dripping extra ghee over the top. Auntie Fatima has made this recipe the same way her whole life; the only difference is she now does it over a gas fire and not a real one.

This was by far one of the hardest dishes to recreate; trying to mimic the combination of beef and fresh milk left me with many curdled meals! But we got there in the end, in the simplest and most delicious way. Whenever you make it, think of Auntie Fatima and all my favourite people in beautiful Dhofar. Serve with white rice and extra ghee.

Heat the ghee and onion in a medium-sized saucepan over a medium–high heat. Sauté the onion for 10 minutes until beginning to turn golden at the edges, then add the beef strips. Continue to fry for another couple of minutes until the onion has browned.

Add 250ml (1 cup plus 1 tbsp) of water, along with the garlic and ginger pastes. Bring to the boil, then cover with a lid and cook over a high heat for 45 minutes until the beef is cooked through and softened.

Now reduce the heat to low and carefully add your double cream, adding it a little at a time and stirring all the while so it doesn't curdle.

Once all the cream is added, stir in the spices and sugar. Bring the mixture to a very gentle simmer and leave for 10 minutes, uncovered.

Stir in the salt, then add your spinach and leave for a further 5 minutes.

Serve with fresh, tasty ghee, drizzled over the top in true Dhofari style.

Gola wa Asal

Fenugreek Pancakes with Honey & Pink Peppercorns

Makes 20

160g (scant 1⅓ cups) plain
    (all-purpose) flour
2 tsp ground fenugreek
2 tsp caster (superfine) sugar
2 tbsp melted ghee
honey, for drizzling
pink peppercorns, crushed,
    for sprinkling

Gola wa asal are mini honey pancakes, also known as *quroos*, which means "round" in Arabic. Across Oman, there is a tradition that when a woman has just given birth, she is fed these pancakes for 40 days. The idea stems from the fact that she needs to be nourished and looked after in order to be able to feed her baby – and it seems like pancakes, lots of honey or date molasses and ghee are key. Some families I have spent time with add *helba* (the Arabic word for fenugreek), which is said to help women produce breast milk.

My friend Rahma took me to visit her sister Nouf, who lives in a village called Ibri. Nouf and her husband showed me how they make and serve these pancakes, in a style known as *shoub*. After we had cooked the pancakes, Nouf added them to a bowl, drizzled over lots of date molasses and some fresh melted ghee, then added a sprinkling of black pepper before mashing them up.

The fenugreek brings a nutty maple aroma and taste, while the pepper with the honey creates an unusual yet fascinating flavour. I chose to use pink peppercorns to give a hint of spice with some sourness, complementing the sweetness of the honey beautifully.

In a large bowl, combine the flour, fenugreek and sugar with 275ml (generous 1 cup) of water. Whisk until smooth.

Heat 1 tablespoon of the ghee in a large frying pan over a medium–high heat. Once the ghee begins to spread out, the pan is hot enough to add the batter.

Using a ladle, spoon in enough batter to make a 7.5cm (3in) circle. These pancakes are small and not too thick. Add as many as you can fit into your pan, then cook for 2–3 minutes until the bottoms are golden brown and the tops look mostly dry.

Flip them over, pressing down slightly with your spatula, then leave them to cook for 1 minute on the other side. Keep the cooked pancakes warm while you repeat with the remaining batter.

Serve drizzled with honey and sprinkled with crushed peppercorns.

Sewiyya/ Tambi/Balaleet

Sweet Cardamom Saffron
Vermicelli with an Omelette

Serves 4

2 pinches of saffron strands
140g (¾ cup minus 2 tsp) caster
    (superfine) sugar
100g (3½oz) raisins
1 tsp ground cardamom
100ml (scant ½ cup) vegetable oil
    or ghee
200g (7oz) long wheat vermicelli
50g (1¾oz) toasted cashews,
    roughly chopped (optional)

For the omelette
3 medium eggs
20g (¾oz) parsley, finely chopped
1 shallot, finely chopped
pinch of salt
1 tbsp salted butter

Known as *sewiyya* in Oman, *tambi* in Zanzibar and *balaleet* across the Gulf, this is a very traditional dish for all of us, made in various ways. At home in Portsmouth, I grew up having it mainly the Zanzibari way, which didn't include an omelette. Sometimes, one of Bibi's friends, Bibi Shuruk, would make us a different version that was baked like a cake, but bound together with coconut milk. When I started visiting my father's family in Oman, I discovered this version. I remember feeling so bamboozled eating it this way for the first time – now I love it. This makes for a fun and different breakfast, while without the egg, it can be a delicious light dessert or sweet daytime snack.

Using a pestle and mortar, grind the saffron with 1 teaspoon of the sugar until fine.

Tip into a large bowl and add 375ml (generous 1½ cups) of boiling water, along with the raisins, cardamom and remaining sugar. Leave to sit.

Heat the oil in a deep frying pan or saucepan over a high heat. Add the vermicelli and cashews and then fry. As it begins to sizzle, use a wooden spoon to break it up slightly. You don't want tiny pieces, but if the vermicelli strands stay at full length, it will be hard to eat. Make sure the vermicelli is well coated in the oil, and continue to fry for about 10 minutes until browned.

Pour the water and raisin mixture into the pan and bring to the boil, then reduce the heat to low–medium. Partially cover the pan with a lid and leave to simmer for about 20 minutes until all the water has evaporated.

Meanwhile, make the omelette. In a bowl, whisk together the eggs, parsley, shallot and salt. Melt the butter in a frying pan over a medium-high heat, then pour in the egg mixture and cook until the omelette is done to your liking.

Once everything is ready, tip the vermicelli on to a large plate, then place the omelette on top and serve.

Luqaimat/ Kaimati

Fried Dumplings in Lemon & Saffron Syrup

Serves 6–8

250g (1¾ cups + 2 tbsp) plain
(all-purpose) flour
50g (generous ⅓ cup) rice flour
50g (scant ¼ cup) plain yogurt
7g (scant ¼oz) fast-action dried
yeast (1 packet)
1 litre (4⅓ cups) vegetable oil, for
deep-frying

For the syrup

200g (1 cup) caster
(superfine) sugar
good pinch of saffron strands
juice of ½ lemon

Luqaimat in Arabic literally means "little bites", and that is exactly what these are. With a crunchy exterior and pillowy interior, these small, sweet spiced bites are found all over the Gulf, Middle East and Swahili coast (the Swahili word is *kaimati*), and also in Turkey and Greece. The Zanzibari version – or maybe it's just my mum and Bibi's version – uses rice flour, which gives the bites a delicate yet hard exterior, whereas those found in Oman and the Gulf tend to be more cake-like and soft. These are an essential part of Ramadan. We rarely make them at any other time of the year, but there is just something about that month that has you craving certain cultural comforts. Nowadays in Oman, you can find *luqaimat* drizzled with chocolate or melted cheese, but spiced and flavoured syrups are always my favourite accompaniment. We usually switch up the syrup flavours depending on our moods, using orange essence or juice, rose water, cardamom, saffron and lemon, so feel free to experiment. The only rule is that you should always have hot *luqaimat* and room-temperature syrup!

Begin by making the syrup. Combine all the syrup ingredients in a small saucepan, then add 170ml (scant ¾ cup) of water and place over a high heat. Once the mixture begins to bubble, let it boil for exactly 10 minutes, then remove from the heat and leave to cool completely.

To make the dumplings, combine all the ingredients (except the oil) in a large bowl. Add 200ml (scant 1 cup) of warm water and whisk until smooth. Cover the bowl with cling film (plastic wrap) and leave to rise for at least 1 hour until the batter has at least doubled in size and has bubbles on the top.

Once the batter has risen, heat the oil in a deep saucepan over a high heat. Test the oil temperature by dropping a little bit of the batter into the pan; if it rises right away, the oil is ready.

Using a teaspoon, scoop up some of the batter and drop it into the pan. Continue, dropping more dollops of batter into the pan (depending on the size of your pan, you'll probably need to work in batches to avoid overcrowding). Let them fry for 3–4 minutes until golden. Pay attention to the heat as the *luqaimat* balls cook; you want the oil to be hot, but not so hot that they change colour too quickly. My mum says the best way to cook these is to keep the oil at a medium–high heat so that they change colour gradually and stay crunchier for longer, but you will have to keep adjusting the heat to achieve this.

Once the first batch is ready, transfer the fried *luqaimat* balls to a strainer to drain off the excess oil while you get started on the next batch. After about 30 seconds of draining, while they are still hot, drop them into the syrup pan and carefully swirl them around to fully coat. Let them sit in the syrup for around 1 minute, then transfer to a bowl to serve.

Sah wa Samen/Tende ya Kusonga

Fennel & Sesame Date Bars

Makes 30

1.1kg (2½lb) pitted dates
1 tsp freshly ground cardamom
150ml (⅔ cup) vegetable oil or
    ghee, plus extra for moulding
30g (1oz) fennel seeds
40g (scant 1½oz) sesame seeds

Across Oman, when people offer you different sweets with your coffee, you'll always find these little date bar squares among them. They are really addictive and are also a good way to use up the not-so-good dates. *Sah wa samen* is the Arabic name, which translates as "dates with ghee", while *tende ya kusonga* is the Swahili name, meaning "dates that are beaten" – in case you couldn't tell, we keep the names of dishes very simple! My mum loves to make lots of these, wrap them nicely and give them out as little gifts. She sometimes cheats and does them in the microwave. While I have used seeds in this recipe, you can also add cashews or almonds.

Line a baking tray with baking parchment (parchment paper).

Place the dates in a non-stick saucepan over a high heat and sprinkle over the cardamom. Using a wooden spoon, break up the dates, just to help separate them and allow them to heat up evenly. Once you start to see steam and hear a slight sizzle, begin mixing and smashing them with the wooden spoon. Reduce the heat to medium–high and keep cooking for 5 minutes, keeping that constant mixing going.

Once you can see the texture changing and the dates starting to soften and stick together, add a third of the oil or ghee. Stir this in, and the mixture will slowly start to loosen. Repeat with another third of the oil or ghee, and once that's combined, add the rest. By this time, you should have been stirring and beating for another 6 minutes, and you will be left with a very smooth, big ball of dates. It won't spread out.

Add the fennel and sesame seeds and continue to beat and mix until combined.

Once you are happy with the distribution of the seeds, tip the mixture into the prepared baking tray. Drizzle some oil on the back of a metal spoon and begin pressing the mixture down with it into an even layer. The easiest way to do this is to smack the mixture with the spoon – my mum says it's the only way to get it smooth and stop everything from sticking.

Once you have spread it out evenly, the mixture should be at least 3–4cm (1¼–1¾ in) thick. Take a small, sharp knife and cut it into 30 diamond-shaped pieces. Don't worry if the knife won't go all the way through; just score it as deeply as you can.

Leave overnight to harden, then cut through the scored lines the next day. These will keep for up to a month in an airtight container, and are perfect to bring out as a snack when guests come over.

Date Stone Coffee

Makes 10 servings

75 date stones (about 40g/scant 1½oz), washed
1 tsp ground ginger
1 tsp ground cinnamon
date syrup or honey (optional), to sweeten

This recipe involves a lot of commitment to eating dates, but if you're into dates and you love coffee, you'll love this! Back in the day, Omanis, especially in the south, would consume date stone coffee, which was introduced by people who had settled in Oman from Yemen. It became known as "poor man's coffee", and offered an alternative for those who couldn't obtain coffee beans. Today, if you're lucky, you can still pick it up in markets in Salalah. I am not a fan of coffee or tea, but this, I am on board with. My mum says it tastes a lot like traditional Omani coffee, which is on the weaker side, but without the same bitterness. Without getting into the science or trying to be your nutritionist, date stones are super good for you! They're anti-inflammatory, and contain antioxidants and a load of other great stuff, so definitely worth a go if you're looking for a caffeine-free energy booster. You can switch up the spices in this drink; my mum likes to add cardamom or saffron. I grind the spices with the date stones, but my mum prefers to grind the stones on their own and then add the spices when brewing, as this gives you freedom to experiment.

Preheat the oven to 200°C (180°C fan/400°F/Gas 6).

Arrange the date stones on a baking tray and roast for 30 minutes, then leave to cool.

Tip the roasted stones into a blender, or a spice or coffee grinder – just something that can give you a fine blend. Add the spices and grind to a fine powder (if you prefer, you can add the spices to the pan when brewing, as my mum does).

Store your date stone coffee powder in a sterilised, airtight container in a dry, dark cupboard for up to 1 month.

To brew and serve, boil around 2 teaspoons of the ground date mixture with 250ml (1 cup plus 1 tbsp) of water in a saucepan over a medium–high heat. Simmer for around 10 minutes, then leave it to rest for 2–4 minutes.

We serve this in little Arabic coffee cups, about the same size as an espresso cup. Sweeten with date syrup or honey to taste, or serve it as it is.

Dried Lime
& Mint Spritz

Serves 2

15g (½oz) mint leaves, plus a few
    sprigs to serve
handful of ice cubes
500ml (generous 2 cups)
    sparkling water

For the dried lime syrup
(makes 375ml/1½ cups)
5 dried limes, about 25g
    (scant 1 oz)
150g (¾ cup) caster
    (superfine) sugar

Dried lime tea is a major thing in Oman and Bahrain. When visiting people's homes, you will often be welcomed with a cup of it. Although it's quite bitter, it is served alongside some sugar or honey to make it more palatable. While I am not a fan of hot drinks, I decided to take the same recipe and create this play on a virgin mojito – although if you prefer a tipple, this would also pair perfectly with rum! If you want to keep it as a tea, follow the same method, minus the sugar, then sweeten to taste when serving.

Start by making the dried lime syrup. Crush the limes slightly to just open them up (don't worry if they break apart) then place in a small saucepan, along with 500ml (generous 2 cups) of still water and the sugar. Bring to the boil over a high heat and boil for exactly 10 minutes, then remove from the heat and leave to cool completely.

To make the drink, crush the mint leaves in the bottom of a cocktail shaker, then add around 140ml (scant ⅔ cup) of the syrup, along with some ice. Shake vigorously, then strain into two tumblers. Add some ice cubes and a couple of mint sprigs, then pour over the sparkling water and serve.

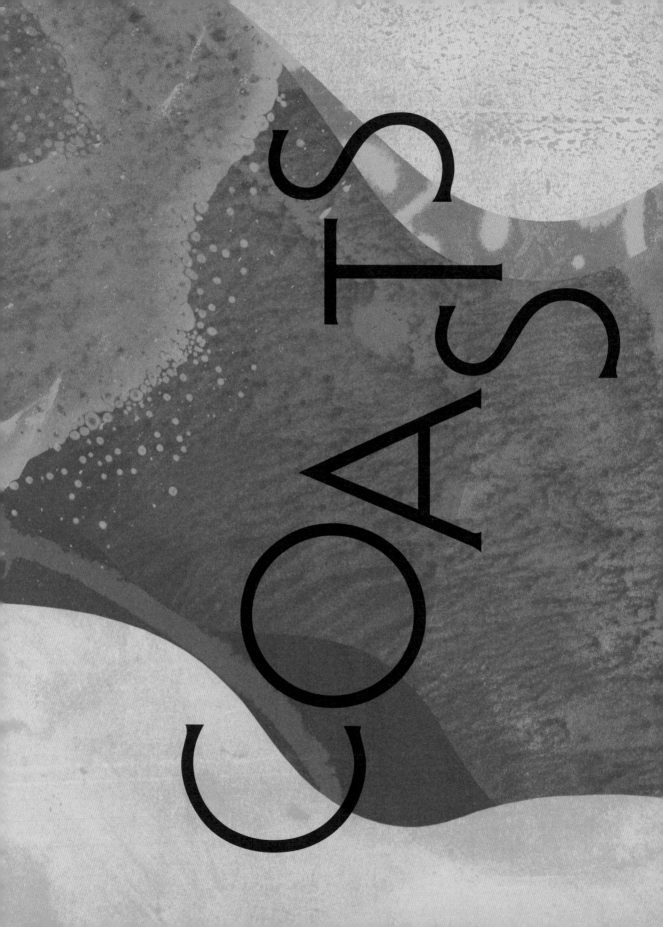

COASTS

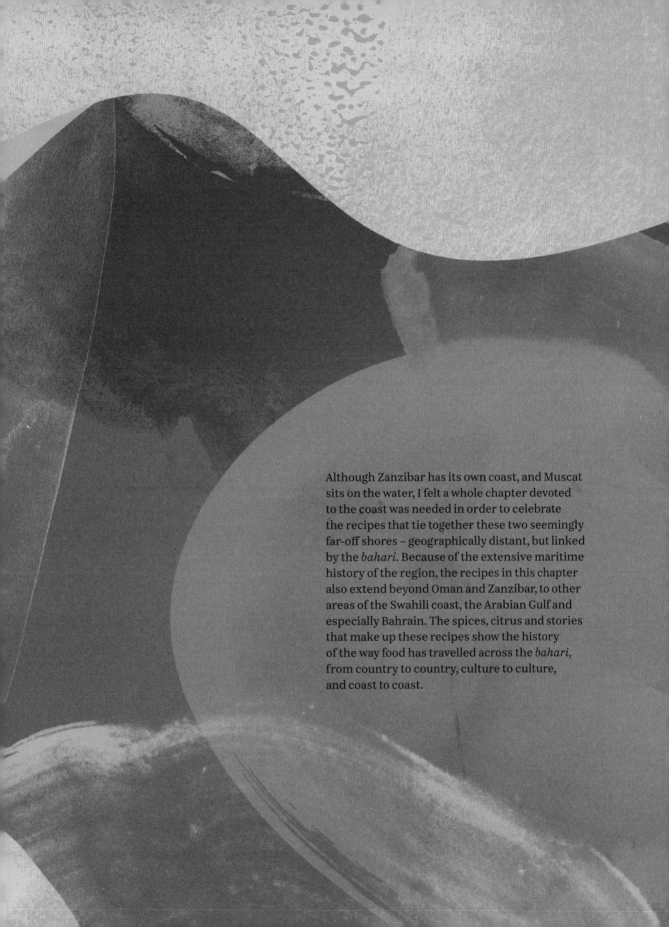

Although Zanzibar has its own coast, and Muscat sits on the water, I felt a whole chapter devoted to the coast was needed in order to celebrate the recipes that tie together these two seemingly far-off shores – geographically distant, but linked by the *bahari*. Because of the extensive maritime history of the region, the recipes in this chapter also extend beyond Oman and Zanzibar, to other areas of the Swahili coast, the Arabian Gulf and especially Bahrain. The spices, citrus and stories that make up these recipes show the history of the way food has travelled across the *bahari*, from country to country, culture to culture, and coast to coast.

Habbar
Bil-Tamar

Date Squid Salad

Serves 4–5

500g (1lb 2oz) squid or cuttlefish
1 small red onion, thinly sliced
1 tbsp olive oil

For the marinade
100ml (scant ½ cup) date syrup
2 tbsp olive oil
4 tsp red wine vinegar
2 tsp ground cinnamon
2 tsp ground ginger
2 tsp black pepper
sea salt, to taste, plus extra
    to serve

For the vinaigrette
juice of 1 large orange
juice of 1 lemon
1 tbsp apple cider vinegar
2 pinches of sea salt
2 tbsp extra virgin olive oil

For the salad
½ cucumber, sliced
4 sweet baby red peppers, sliced
seeds of 1 pomegranate
60g (2oz) rocket (arugula) leaves
6 Swiss chard stalks, finely
    chopped
1 grapefruit, peeled and cut into
    segments
100g (3½oz) pine nuts, toasted
100g (3½oz) feta, crumbled

During my work on this book, I've found Omani seafood recipes the most challenging to replicate. If anything, this dish has taught me to really appreciate freshly caught seafood, because the flavour is truly unmatched. This recipe is inspired by one shared with me by an Omani fisherman called Mohammed Al Riyami, who I met at the Mutrah fish market. He was selling humongous pieces of squid, and his hands were covered in their ink. It was the first time I had seen such big pieces; I felt like a kid in a candy store, and just wanted to buy them all. Omanis don't often cook with squid, so I asked him what he used it for, and he told me fishermen and their families cook squid in dates. They leave the dates and squid to stew for at least an hour until the squid has turned red, adding very little seasoning – usually just a bit of garlic and salt. It creates a thick sauce, and they have it with rice or bread. I must have spent so much money on squid in an attempt to recreate that recipe, but I just couldn't yield the same flavour. Even when I got the flavour working, I felt it was just missing something, and the texture wasn't quite right. So although I really wanted you to have a date squid recipe, because it's something I haven't really seen before, I decided to do things a little differently. I also love using the same marinade for pieces of white fish, which I then grill, air fry or bake.

In a large bowl, combine all the marinade ingredients and whisk together. Add your pieces of squid and the red onion slices and stir to coat, then cover with cling film (plastic wrap) and leave to marinate in the fridge for at least 2–3 hours, but ideally overnight.

Once marinated, place a griddle or frying pan over a high heat and brush with the 1 tablespoon of olive oil. You want the pan to be as hot as possible, so test with a piece of onion; if it begins to sizzle instantly, then pour all the squid mixture into the pan. Sauté for around 4 minutes – you don't want to overcook the squid.

Once cooked, reduce the heat to low and remove the squid pieces, setting them aside in a bowl to cool. Sauté the rest of the marinade-and-onion mix in the pan for a further couple of minutes, then pour the mixture into a large jar and leave to cool completely.

Once everything is cool, take your jar of marinade-and-onion mix and add the vinaigrette ingredients. Cover with a lid and shake well to make your dressing. Chill until needed.

To serve, combine all the salad ingredients in a salad bowl. Add your squid pieces to the salad and sprinkle over some sea salt to taste. Just before serving, pour over some of the dressing, or serve it at the table for everyone to pour over themselves. Any leftover dressing can be stored in the fridge for 3–4 days.

Coasts

Bajiya ya dengu

Black-eyed Bean & Mung Bean Falafel

Makes 30–35 pieces

170g (6oz) black-eyed beans
   (black-eyed peas)
200g (7oz) mung beans
1 garlic clove
salt, to taste
2 green chillies (optional)
30g (1oz) coriander (cilantro)
3 large onions, 2 roughly chopped
   and 1 finely chopped
1 litre (4⅓ cups) vegetable or
   sunflower oil, for deep-frying
1 heaped tsp baking powder

Tip:

The *bajiya* mixture can be frozen
once blended, and defrosted when
you want to fry.

Whenever I tell people I'm from the Middle East or Oman, most will instantly ask me if I know how to make great falafel. I once attended a talk at the British Library on food that connected us to our roots, and the wonderful Imad, from Imad's Syrian Kitchen in London, spoke about how cooking falafel helped him survive in Calais as a refugee after fleeing Syria. The dish acted as his form of communication and currency. This reminded me that making generalisations about cultures suppresses our stories and history, especially when we have come from colonised and conflicted countries. Food is our resistance and a way of holding on to our heritage.

So while we in Oman and Zanzibar do love falafel, we leave it to our neighbours to make, and instead we have *bajiya*, which I guess is similar in terms of its method and ingredients. *Bajiya* comes from the Omani-Zanzibari diaspora, and is seen across other parts of the Swahili coast, made using pulses local to those areas. The word stems from the Hindi word *bhaji*, or "fried vegetable". The Indian community played a big part in the development of many of our fried dishes. Using what they had available on the island, they were able to make these simple *bajiya*. We use black-eyed beans and mung beans, and serve these with a coconut dip called *chatini* (see page 181 for my version).

Soak the black-eyed beans and mung beans in cold water overnight in two separate bowls.

The next day, gently massage the black-eyed beans in their soaking water to help release their skins. The skin should float to the top; remove as much as you can, as this will stop the *bajiya* from absorbing too much oil. Drain the beans really well and pat dry to remove any excess water.

Tip both types of beans into a food processor, along with the garlic, salt, chillies, coriander and roughly chopped onions. Blitz until the mixture is smooth and the beans have completely broken down. Set aside.

Pour the oil into a deep frying pan or wok over a high heat.

While the oil is heating, stir the baking powder and finely chopped onion into the *bajiya* mixture, combining well. This will help them become super fluffy and round.

Using a tablespoon or ice-cream scoop, plop some of the mixture into the pan; if it floats instantly and begins to sizzle, the oil is hot enough for frying. Add as many balls of *bajiya* mixture to the oil as you can, leaving enough room for them to move around.

Fry for 4–5 minutes, making sure to keep turning them so they brown evenly. You're looking for a deep brown colouring on the outside. Once cooked, transfer the *bajiya* to a plate lined with kitchen paper (paper towels) to drain the excess oil while you fry the next batch, and serve.

Baharat Spice Blend

Makes 600g (1lb 5oz)

100g (3½oz) whole black
    peppercorns
70g (scant 2½ oz) cardamom pods
40g (scant 1½oz) whole nutmeg
100g (3½oz) cinnamon sticks
50g (1¾oz) whole cloves
150g (5oz) cumin seeds
100g (3½oz) coriander seeds

Baharat is Arabic for "mixed blend", and that's literally what this spice mix is. Every family will have their own version that symbolises their background and roots. Mine is Bibi's recipe, which she learned from her mum. In Zanzibar, they call it garam masala, as it's more or less the same as that. I swear by this spice blend; I could live without every other spice, except this. When a meal isn't going right, I add a dash; when I can't be bothered to think about what to eat or how to play with flavours, I use this. It always saves the day, and makes recipes taste great. All the recipes in this book that mention baharat spice blend use this version, so if I were you, I would make a batch and keep it in the cupboard for whenever you whip out *Bahari*.

Preheat the oven to 180°C (160°C fan/350°F/Gas 4) and line a baking tray with baking parchment.

Combine all the spices on the prepared baking tray and toast in the oven for 15 minutes until the spices are releasing their aromas and beginning to slightly darken.

Remove from the oven and leave to cool, then add to a spice grinder or blender and grind down to a fine powder.

Store in a sterilised airtight jar. It should keep for a year, but I'm hoping you'll use it up way before that!

Kachumbar

Mango & Onion Salad

Serves 4–5

1 large onion, finely diced
salt, to taste
1 ripe mango, finely diced
seeds of 1 pomegranate
½ cucumber, finely diced
2 tomatoes, finely diced
15g (½oz) coriander (cilantro),
   finely chopped
juice of 1½ lemons

Kachumbar, sometimes known as *kachumbari*, derives from India, but made its way to the Swahili coast. There are variations, but the principle idea is to have lots of onions and to cut the salad ingredients into very small pieces. *Kachumbar* was my first introduction to salad; we had it with every rice meal when I was a kid, and it was something my cousins and I would fight for at the table. The person who got the last portion also got to drink the lemon juice, which was my favourite part. I remember when I would visit my school friends at their homes, I was so confused as to why their salads were just lettuce leaves and maybe some tomato and cucumber, but never any lemon. At the same time, they found me odd for having lemon and onions in my salad! I love to add fruits to this salad; Bibi has always added grapes and apples, while my mum opts for mango. My addition has always been pomegranate seeds, of course.

Soak the diced onion in a bowl of water with a pinch of salt and let it sit for at least 10 minutes. This removes the bitterness.

Combine the mango, pomegranate seeds, cucumber, tomatoes and coriander in a bowl, then drain the onion and stir this in, too.

Squeeze in the lemon juice and season with salt to your taste, then serve as a side dish (see page 161).

SUR

The coastal town of Sur is the one Omani city that brings me the summery seaside-town vibes I grew up with in Portsmouth. It may be missing the 99 flake ice-cream cones, fairground, pebbled beaches and pier, but Sur is my happy place, my comfort.

As you emerge from the mountains into the start of the city, despite having to first overlook the rather protruding and obnoxious gasfield, the meandering road will guide you to an idyllic harbour where the hues of the sky meet the ocean. The striking architecture and deep tones of teak-wood dhows floating in the bay (pictured overleaf) bring a sense of peace and tranquillity.

As a child, this was one of the first towns I ever visited outside of Muscat. My mum had always wanted to take me to a place called Ras Al Jinz, a magical turtle reserve in Sur, where at night, the sea phosphorus swooshes in against the shore, lighting up the beach. This is where the turtles lay their eggs, and if you're lucky you may see hundreds of hatchlings scurry off into the ocean to begin their lives. I've seen it happen once, and it's nothing short of a Disney film. Perhaps this is why Sur holds such a sense of nostalgia for me, but I think it's also because of the ancestral history connecting me to the town, thanks to the maritime trade between India and Zanzibar.

Sur was once a bustling port town and played a pivotal role in the country's trade. The town has one of the oldest ports in the world, and since the sixth century, it has been the pinnacle for connecting Africa with India, South East Asia, the Arabian Peninsula and Persia, with up to 150 ships entering the port every day until about 100 years ago. I remember my friend's Auntie Samiya telling me the reason they eat so much fish in the city isn't because it's by the

sea, but because the Arab Sea brings the tastiest fish you can find in the region. Little did I realise then that Sur is where all three seas meet – Persian Gulf, Arabian Sea and Indian Ocean – bringing you the best of each, so of course it holds the finest delicacies of the *bahari*.

The port began to decline when the Suez Canal opened up in 1869 and created easier access to the rest of the world. Although trade was forgotten about, the building of dhows continued, and Sur has become famous for the handcrafting of these incredible vessels (pictured overleaf). Aside from that, however, Suris (the name given to people from Sur) have happily nestled away in their town with possibly the most glorious food in the country – food that pays homage to varied influences brought from their maritime history.

I have been lucky enough to spend time in Suri homes thanks to my wonderful friend Sara Al Hashar, who opened up doors to aunts, uncles and grandparents so I could taste and revel in their dishes. I was astounded. Suris have undeniably held on to recipes, methods and flavours from Africa and India. They eat coconut in sweet ways, just as we do in Zanzibar, and they concoct everything in huge amounts of chilli, which they tell me is predominantly down to the Indian influences. The majority of their dishes are seafood-based, and from everything I experienced, it almost seems like their way of continuing their maritime legacy.

Coasts

S'aid Mgalay

Auntie Samiya's Suri
Fried Fish

Serves 2

3 tbsp garlic paste
3 pinches of sea salt flakes,
    or to taste
2 tbsp chilli flakes or 1 tbsp hot
    chilli powder
2 sea bass fillets (skin on), about
    300–350g (10–12oz), halved
4 tbsp vegetable oil
juice of 1 lemon

For the dry spice mix
1 tbsp ground ginger
1 tbsp ground cinnamon
1 tbsp ground black pepper
1 tbsp ground cumin

While there are so many recipes I want to share from Sur, the most well known is this dish. *S'aid mgalay* translates as "fried fish"; in Arabic, the word for "fish" is usually *samak*, but the word *s'aid* means "to go hunting or fishing" and Suris don't hunt for any other animal except fish. This fried fish recipe also connects me to Zanzibar and Portsmouth. It is a Bibi special, something she has always made at home. Anytime she hears I am heading down to the fishmongers, she will tell me to bring her back some sea bass so she can fry it. Auntie Samiya taught me some of her secrets, and I've also brought in some of Bibi's methods to create this version.

In a small bowl, mix together the garlic paste, salt and chilli, then spread this paste evenly over both sides of the sea bass fillets in a thick layer. Marinate in the fridge for at least 1 hour.

Meanwhile, combine the dry spice mix ingredients in a small bowl and set aside.

When you are ready to fry your fish, heat 2 tablespoons of the oil in a frying pan over a high heat. Sprinkle about 1 teaspoon of the dry spice mix on each side of each fillet, making sure that you press it down so it sticks to the garlic marinade.

Now place two of the pieces of fish in the hot frying pan; they should sizzle as soon as they hit the pan. Fry for 2–4 minutes on each side, depending on how cooked you like your fish.

Once cooked, transfer to a plate and squeeze some lemon over each side (Auntie Samiya says this is the key to a great Suri fried fish). Repeat with the remaining fish and oil. Serve with rice and a leafy green salad.

Cooking notes:

This will work with a few different types of fish; just don't choose anything too flaky, as you need it to hold together. If you can get fresh local tuna, use it.

It gets smoky in the kitchen with this one as you keep it on a high heat, so I suggest you open the windows.

Samaki wa Kupaka

Basted Snapper
with Coconut, Lemon
& Turmeric Sauce

Serves 4

1 whole red snapper, about
1kg (2¼lb), cleaned
(I keep the head on)

For the marinade

1 tbsp baharat spice blend (see
page 120)

1 tsp salt

1 tsp chilli powder

2 tsp garlic paste

1 tsp ginger paste

juice of ½ lemon

4 tbsp neutral oil, such as
light vegetable oil

For the sauce

2 × 400ml (14fl oz) cans of
coconut milk

1 onion, thinly sliced

1 tsp baharat spice blend

1 tsp ground turmeric

juice of 1–2 lemons

1 fresh green chilli,
roughly chopped

salt, to taste

The school I went to was about a five-minute walk from the dockyard in Portsmouth in the UK. At least once a week, my mum would pick me up and we'd walk down to the fishmongers together after school. I never knew which day we would go, but the minute my mum told me, I would be over the moon. I must have been an odd seven-year-old – I don't remember any of my friends ever being so excited to go and buy fish! The shop, known as Viviers, had a strong smell of the sea, and was always very wet inside. Depending on the season, we would pick up fresh crabs, prawns or mussels – and always a sea bass for Bibi and Babu, as it was Bibi's favourite. The crabs would petrify me, as you could see them wriggling around in the container. After collecting our order, we would stroll across to a man who sold fish from his van and grab two polystyrene cups of pickled anchovies so that I could gobble them down as we walked back to the car.

The evenings following these trips were always full of anticipation as I eagerly awaited dinner. My mum would cook everything we'd bought using this recipe, and then she would take a piece of striped plastic sheet that came off a roll and lay it on the living room floor. She'd give me an apron to wear, and then we would sit down opposite one another and dig straight into the pan. It was our special ritual. We probably had many great meals during the week, but this is the one I've always remembered.

This is very much a Zanzibari recipe, and it's also found along the Swahili coast, particularly in Kenya and Tanzania, although I would say it's made more often with chicken on the mainland. I personally think this dish is a beautiful representation of Zanzibari cuisine; it's one of those recipes people try for the first time and remember forever. We usually make this with sea bass, but salmon and bream work well too and here, I've used snapper because I love the taste. I like to serve this with white rice, crispy onions and my Kachumbar salad (see page 121).

Begin by making the marinade. Combine all the marinade ingredients in a bowl until you have a loose paste.

Make 3–4 slits on each side of the fish, then coat your fish with the paste, making sure you work it into the slits. If there is any extra paste, just pour it all over the top. Leave to marinate for at least an hour in the fridge.

Recipe continues overleaf

When you're ready to cook, preheat your grill to its highest heat, then line a high-sided baking tray with foil. Place the fish in the prepared tray and grill for 10–13 minutes until the top of the fish is cooked. (Make sure not to place the fish too close to the heat or it may catch.)

While the fish is grilling, make the sauce. In a saucepan, combine the coconut milk, onion, baharat and turmeric with the juice of 1 lemon, then add the chilli. Season to taste, then bring to the boil over a high heat. Once boiling, reduce the heat to medium and leave to simmer while you finish cooking the fish. Taste for lemon, and add a little more lemon juice if needed; you want it tangy but not overpowering.

Turn the fish over and cook on the other side for another 10–13 minutes. Once this is done, spoon a ladleful of the coconut sauce over the fish and return it to the grill for a minute or so until the sauce bubbles. It should deepen in colour and slightly thicken. Repeat with a couple more ladlefuls; you want to use up about three quarters of the sauce, then keep the rest for serving.

Transfer the fish to a plate and pour over the remaining sauce. Serve with your chosen accompaniments and eat right away.

Tip:

Once you are familiar with this dish and its flavours, you can adapt it the way my mother does with crab, mussels and prawns instead of fish. When using shellfish, you essentially stew them with all the marinading spices and ingredients to form the sauce.

Bahraini Tikka

Makes about 15 skewers

600g (1lb 5oz) beef tenderloin,
    cut into 2.5cm (1in) cubes
3 tbsp garlic paste
2 tbsp ground dried lime
½ tsp ground ginger
1 tbsp freshly ground black
    pepper
1 tsp salt
1 tsp ground cumin
3 tbsp vegetable oil, plus extra
    for brushing

Both my mother and father's families have ancestry from Bahrain. In Oman, people with this lineage are known as "Bahranis" or "Baharnas".

Having such a small and close community means we are all familiar with each family's characteristics and cuisines, and so Bahraini tikka is well known and loved among our community in Muscat. There is only one place in Muscat that does a good one; the shop mainly makes shuwarmas, and is called Antalya after the city in Turkey, but nestled in the back is a man who makes excellent tikka: succulent, chargrilled skewers with a tender tang. I first tried it at my cousin Narjis's house. Her mum had ordered some in, and couldn't believe I hadn't experienced it before. I knew I had to learn how to make it, and so I asked my friend Hussain's mother to share her recipe with me. While she "cheats" with some MSG lemon flavouring in addition to the dried lime, I think I've managed to work it to perfection!

It is essential that you eat this meat with bread, as the dried lime comes in very sharp if eaten on its own. While cooking these on coal helps to bring a sense of smokiness to the sharp citrus taste, cooking the meat in a griddle pan on the hob will also work beautifully, as you'll retain more of the juices. Serve with flatbread, hummus, raw onions, tomatoes, watercress or lettuce, fresh chilli and sliced oranges.

Combine all the ingredients in a large bowl and massage with your hands to make sure the marinade has coated the meat well.

Cover the bowl with cling film (plastic wrap) and place in the fridge for at least 1 hour, but no more than 3–4 hours, as the acidity from the lime will tenderise the meat too much.

If you're using an outdoor grill or barbecue, or an indoor grill, preheat it to medium–high. If you're using a griddle pan, heat over a medium–high heat and brush generously with oil.

Thread the beef chunks on to skewers, adding five chunks to each one. Cook the beef for 3–4 minutes on each side, leaving it slightly pink in the middle but nicely charred on the outside.

Serve the tikka with your chosen accompaniments. If you cooked it in a griddle pan, drizzle over any excess juices from the pan to serve.

Tips:

Add an extra tablespoon of the dried lime powder if you like it sour.

This recipe works best with black lime powder (see page 37).

Machboos

Chicken, Tomato & Dried Lime One-Pot Rice Dish

Serves 5–6

6 tbsp vegetable oil

1 onion, chopped

3 garlic cloves or 1 tbsp garlic paste

2 cinnamon sticks

8 cardamom pods

3 tsp baharat spice blend (see page 120)

2 green chillies (optional), halved or roughly chopped

2 dried limes

2 tbsp tomato purée (paste)

1 chicken, about 1–1.5kg (2¼lb–3lb 3oz), cut into 8 pieces, skin left on or removed according to your preference

3 tomatoes, finely chopped

½ red or green (bell) pepper, chopped

pinch of salt

600g (3 cups) basmati rice

50g (1¾oz) blanched almonds (optional)

10g (¼ oz) coriander (cilantro), finely chopped

seeds of ½ pomegranate (optional)

Across most of the Gulf and in a few other Arab countries, this dish is known as *machboos*, meaning "to compress", as the ingredients are cooked in one pot, with the meat compressed beneath the rice. In Saudi Arabia, it's also known as *kabsa*, deriving from the root word *kabs*, which is the act of putting rice on the meat once it's cooked. My mum has always been fond of making this dish. The traditional method takes much longer, as you would normally fry each element separately, but my mum also loves to make cooking quick and easy, so she taught me a simplified version that still yields the same taste. This is most commonly made with chicken, and that's my favourite way to eat it, but you can easily substitute chicken for vegetables or lamb.

Heat 3 tablespoons of the oil in a large saucepan over a low–medium heat. Add the onion and sauté for around 5 minutes until turning slightly brown at the edges. Add the garlic, spices, chillies (if using) and dried limes. Stir well and fry for a further 2–4 minutes, then stir in the tomato purée.

Lay the chicken pieces in the pan and sear for 6–10 minutes on each side, then add the tomatoes and pepper, followed by 1 litre (4⅓ cups) of water. Season with a pinch of salt, then increase the heat to medium–high. Cover with a lid and leave to bubble away for 20 minutes, or until the chicken is cooked through.

Once the chicken is cooked, add the rice, along with the remaining 3 tablespoons of oil. Reduce the heat to the lowest setting, then securely wrap a clean tea towel around your saucepan lid and place it on top of the pan – this will help create more steam and make your rice extra fluffy. Leave to cook for about 20 minutes.

Meanwhile, toast your almonds in a dry frying pan over a medium heat for about 5 minutes until golden.

Once your rice is cooked, divide the *machboos* between 4 plates. Scatter over the toasted almonds and finish with a sprinkling of fresh coriander and pomegranate seeds.

Chuku Chuku

Unripe Mango & Lemon Chicken Curry in a Hurry

Serves 4

6–8 skinless chicken pieces, about 1–1.5kg (2¼lb–3lb 3oz), ideally on the bone

400g (14oz) can chopped tomatoes

1 tbsp baharat spice blend (see page 120) or garam masala

1 tsp ground turmeric

1 tbsp garlic paste

1 tbsp ginger paste

1 onion, thinly sliced

2 potatoes, peeled and quartered

juice of 2 lemons

1 unripe mango, peeled, stoned and sliced

Chuku chuku (sometimes known on the mainland as *mchuzi wa maje*, or "curry of water") is a Zanzibari curry in a hurry. It's something we have at home often; I could easily make it twice a week, as I love it so much. It always feels like a hug in a bowl for me. It has a very light, soupy consistency that drowns your rice as you eat. Swahili people usually have this with fish, but Bibi never liked it that way, so we always grew up having it with chicken. The whole point of this dish is to make it sour; lemon is key to this, while an unripe mango adds a very sour tang. It's not mandatory, but it just packs in another layer of acidity that you'll love! If you can't get hold of an unripe mango, try adding some sour lime or mango pickle for a similar flavour. Serve with white basmati rice.

Combine all the ingredients except for the mango and lemon juice in a large, deep saucepan. Add 1 litre (4⅓ cups) of water and bring to the boil over a medium–high heat. Reduce the heat to medium and leave to bubble away for 45 minutes until the chicken is cooked through.

Add your lemon juice and mango slices and cook for a further 15 minutes.

Serve with white basmati rice. Simple as that.

Mbaazi

Pigeon peas in Coconut

Serves 2–3

3400g (14oz) can of gungo beans or red kidney beans

400ml (14fl oz) can of coconut milk

1 small onion, thinly sliced

½ tsp ground turmeric

salt, to taste

This is a very typical Swahili dish eaten across the coast. In Kenya, it's made with kidney beans, but we Zanzibaris always use pigeon peas, also known as gungo beans. It is such a simple dish to make. We usually eat it with chapati or rice. This and *mchicha* (see page 159 for my recipe) are the dishes Bibi gets most excited about making for anyone vegan who comes to visit her.

Combine all the ingredients in a medium-sized saucepan over a medium–high heat and leave to simmer for 20 minutes until the coconut has reduced, the peas have softened, and the mixture has come together into a slightly thick sauce.

Serve warm, as a side dish, with rice or some flatbread.

Magole

Savoury Spring Onion
& Green Chilli Pancakes

Makes 8

260g (scant 2 cups) plain
  (all-purpose) flour
1 tsp salt
4 spring onions, finely
  chopped
2 green chillies, finely chopped
1 tbsp vegetable oil, for frying

Magoles are savoury Zanzibari pancakes, sometimes known on other parts of the Swahili coast as *mkate wa maji,* meaning "water bread". They are a typical breakfast pancake for us at home, where we enjoy them with a good drizzle of honey or date syrup.

In a large bowl, combine the flour and salt with 300ml (1¼ cups) of water and whisk until smooth. You're looking for a pourable pancake consistency.

Stir in the spring onions and chilli and mix well.

Heat the oil in a non-stick frying pan over a medium heat. Add a ladleful of the batter, then use the bottom of the ladle to spread it out to form a large circle. Fry for 2 minutes, then flip over to cook on the other side for 2 minutes.

Repeat for the rest of the batter – you will not need to add any more oil to the pan – then serve.

Mkate
wa Ufuta

Sesame Coconut Flatbread

Makes 9–10

650ml (generous 2 ¾ cups) warm
    coconut milk
7g (scant ¼oz) fast-action
    dried yeast (1 packet)
650g (5¼ cups) plain
    (all-purpose) flour
2 tsp salt
2 tbsp salted butter or olive oil,
    plus extra for glazing
sesame seeds, for sprinkling

I call this bread the love child of a Zanzibari and an Italian. It has to be one of my favourite breads to make; it is so easy and fun, and the outcome is heavenly. The consistency of the dough is very similar to focaccia, hence the Italian reference. We make it with coconut milk, which helps with the soft, spongy texture. Although it's traditional to put sesame seeds on top, I play around with the toppings a lot! Sometimes I use za'atar, sometimes harissa chickpeas – really, whatever I fancy, so please have fun with it. My top tip is to use salty butter, and lots of it! When you use it to glaze the freshly cooked bread, it soaks right in and transforms it completely.

Pour the coconut milk into a bowl. Add the yeast and leave to sit for 5 minutes.

In a large bowl or mixer, combine the flour, salt and butter, then add the coconut milk and yeast mixture. Mix to form a loose batter – this will take 10–15 minutes by hand, or 5–6 minutes if using a mixer. I prefer to do this by hand, so you can get the consistency right. The mixture won't come together into a ball of dough like a normal bread. It should be very loose and very smooth, but not too liquid.

Cover the bowl with cling film (plastic wrap) and leave the dough to rise for at least 1½ hours, or until it has doubled in size.

When you're ready to cook, heat an ovenproof frying pan over a medium heat and turn your grill on to high.

Knock back the dough in the bowl and pull with your hands to make sure it's stretchy.

Add a tiny amount of butter or oil to the pan, then grab a handful of the dough. Drop it into the pan and carefully spread it out with your fingers into a circle. You can dip your fingers into water if you find the dough is too sticky; this will also help it spread more easily.

Once you're happy with the shape, sprinkle over some sesame seeds and fry for 4-5 minutes until partly cooked. Ideally, you want the bottom to have slightly browned, and you'll notice it is starting to go dry on top. At this stage, place the pan directly under the grill and allow the top of the bread to cook. After about 1–2 minutes, it will rise slightly, and start to turn golden, at which point you can remove it from the grill. Pay close attention – it may look like nothing has happening for a while, and then suddenly the bread is charred!

Quickly transfer the bread to a plate and, using a pastry brush, brush it with oil or butter so that it can seep through the bread while it is still hot. Repeat for the rest of the dough, then serve.

Tips:

These flatbreads can be enjoyed right away, but are also delicious cold – just make sure to keep them covered, as they'll go hard if left out.

The cooked breads can be frozen for up to a month and reheated in the oven.

Mkate wa Kumina

Sweet Rice & Coconut Bread

Serves 6–8

400g (2 cups) basmati rice
220g (1 cup plus 2 tbsp) caster (superfine) sugar
10 cardamom pods, crushed or ground
14g (scant ½ oz) fast-action dried yeast (2 packets)
400ml (14fl oz) can of coconut milk, warmed
1 egg white
salted or unsalted butter, for greasing and brushing

Mkate wa kumina is Swahili for "pouring bread". Zanzibaris are very literal when it comes to describing things, and this bread is exactly what it sounds like. The mix is like a thick pancake batter that you pour into a frying pan and cook on the hob, before placing under the grill to cook the top. Although we call it a bread, it's more like a cake, and is usually served with tea for dunking, but it's also delicious with coffee or hot chocolate. A similar batter, minus the egg, is also used to make pancakes, which we call *chila* (see page 186 for my recipe), and also to make little balls, which we call *vitumbua*. Those look very similar to Danish *aebleskiver* (apple pancake balls), and I've also heard they make something similar in Thailand and parts of India. I have tried baking this bread in the oven, but I felt it ruined the texture. The mix of the hob and grill makes such a difference. Please note the rice needs to be soaked overnight, and you'll also need a high-powered blender.

Put the rice into a bowl and pour over enough water to cover. Leave to soak overnight, then drain.

Combine all the ingredients except the butter in a bowl, then transfer to a high-powered blender in small batches to blend. You want to blend each batch for about 1–2 minutes, until the rice is very, very fine and completely broken down. The grains should be gone or extremely small.

Combine all the blended mixture in a large bowl, cover with a clean cloth and leave to rise for 1½–2 hours until it has doubled in size and has lots of bubbles on the top.

When you're ready to cook, grease an ovenproof frying pan that's roughly 28cm (11in) in diameter and 5cm (2in) deep (if your pan is smaller, you can just make two smaller breads), then place over a low heat.

Using a ladle, mix the risen batter, then scoop it up from the bottom of the bowl and fill your pan with all the batter. Cover with a lid and leave to cook for 12–15 minutes. You want to cook this as slowly and gently as possible. The slower it cooks, the softer the bread will be, and the more certain you can be that it has cooked through the middle.

Meanwhile, preheat your grill to high.

You'll know the bread is ready when it comes away from the pan and has a slight wobble in the middle. Once it is at this stage, place the pan under the grill for about 10 minutes to cook the top. It should be slightly golden on top and the wobble will be gone.

Remove from the heat and brush with butter, then leave to cool slightly. Turn the bread out on to a large plate and serve warm or cold.

Ndizi Mbivu

Sweet Coconut Plantain Pudding

Serves 2

2 ripe plantains, about 400–500g
    (14oz–1lb 2oz)
50g (¼ cup) caster
    (superfine) sugar
10 cardamom pods, ground
400ml (14fl oz) can of coconut milk

Ndizi mbivu literally means "ripe bananas" in Swahili. However, when someone says it, or *mkono wa tembo* (arm/trunk of an elephant), it actually means they are making this: a very simple Zanzibari/Swahili pudding made from plantain that is boiled in coconut with cardamom, cinnamon or nutmeg. We have always eaten these on their own, but they are also a fabulous addition to pancakes, waffles, ice cream or your morning porridge.

Peel the plantains and quarter them lengthways.

Place the skins, outer-skin down, in a saucepan – this is an old Zanzibari method to stop the plantain from sticking to the pan and burning. Place the plantain flesh on top, then pour over 200ml (scant 1 cup) of water, along with the sugar and cardamom.

Bring to the boil over a high heat. Boil for 15 minutes, then add the coconut milk and continue to simmer on a medium heat for a further 10–15 minutes until the plantains are soft but not mushy and the liquid has thickened.

Serve right away, or save in the fridge for up to 3 days to enjoy with your pancakes, satisfy late-night cravings or liven up your morning porridge (discard the plantain skins at the bottom of the dish).

Mini Basil Pavlovas with Mango Cream

Makes 12 individual pavlovas

25g (scant 1oz) fresh basil leaves
(do not use dried basil!), plus
extra to serve
300g (1½ cups) caster
(superfine) sugar
4 egg whites
1 tsp white vinegar
squeeze of lime juice
20g (¾oz) cornflour (cornstarch)
fresh fruit, such as pomegranates,
berries, fresh mango or
physalis, to garnish

For the mango cream
200ml (scant 1 cup) double
(heavy) cream
160g (5¾oz) mango purée or
2 fresh mangoes, peeled,
stoned and blended

If I were a boy, my name would have been Basil, not because my mum likes the herb, but because in Arabic, it means "brave". She was always confident that she would have a boy, so spent the whole nine months calling me Basil – imagine her reaction when she found out I was a girl!

During her pregnancy, she was addicted to mangoes, and my father would deliver her a couple of boxes every day from his farm so she could devour them. During the mango season, he would take her to a village called Quriyat, which is known for having the sweetest and best mangoes in the country. On one visit, they had taken a walk down the beach and met a little girl named Dina who was fascinated by my mum's big bump. My mum complimented her on her name and said she was having a boy called Basil. This dessert is an ode to my name, and also to my mother's pregnancy cravings, because had she not had them, I probably would have been a girl called Basil.

Preheat the oven to 120°C (100°C fan/215°F/Gas ¼) and line a baking tray with baking parchment (parchment paper).

In a blender, blitz the basil with 250g (1¼ cups) of the sugar so that the basil breaks down and mixes with the sugar.

Add the egg whites, vinegar and lime juice to a mixer, then whisk on a medium–high speed for 8–10 minutes until soft peaks form. At this stage, start adding the remaining 50g (¼ cup) of sugar, 1 teaspoon at a time, still whisking, until the meringue starts to become glossy.

Next, start adding the basil sugar, again, adding it slowly, a little at a time. Once it has all been added, whisk on a high speed for 2–4 minutes until the mixture is very glossy and close to having stiff peaks – you won't get super-stiff peaks like you would when making a normal meringue because of the basil.

Add the cornflour and allow it to incorporate (this will take about 15 seconds), then immediately turn off the machine.

Depending on the style you want, you can either use a spoon to dollop 12 pavlova shapes on to the prepared tray, or use a piping bag to pipe them.

Recipe continues overleaf

Bake for 1½ hours, then switch off the oven and allow the meringues to cool completely inside (I usually leave them overnight). Try to avoid opening the oven door if you can.

To make the mango cream, whip the cream in a mixer until stiff peaks form, then whisk in the mango purée or blended mango. As you do this, the peaks will soften, but the overall mixture will stay thick. Keep the cream refrigerated until you're ready to serve.

To serve, top each meringue with a dollop of cream, then finish with the fresh fruit of your choice, along with a few extra basil leaves.

Cooking notes:

It's best to leave the meringues in the oven to dry out overnight, as they really need that extra time.

I prefer to use mango purée for this recipe, particularly alphonso. It's fine to use fresh alphonso mangoes if in season, but other mangoes tend not to be sweet enough. If you do use a different variety of fresh mango, you will need to add a bit of sugar to taste.

I prefer to make these as individual pavlovas because of the softer texture of the meringue, but you can make one big pavlova if you prefer. It will need to bake for at least 3 hours.

CARDAMOM

If there is one thing we can collectively agree on, it is how traumatising it is to bite into a cardamom pod by mistake. As a child, I wouldn't eat anything cooked with the spice, and continued to resist cardamom-based dishes into my twenties. To me, it always felt like smoked mint and camphor were circulating in my mouth – not the best combination, especially when you consider that camphor is the scent used in the mosque when people die. I remember the smell of camphor circulating in our mosque when my grandfather (Babu) died; the room his body was kept in was being purified with that scent. After that day, a whiff of camphor would make me shudder as I remembered Babu – but interestingly, I found the taste of cardamom didn't bother me anymore. In fact, it began to grow on me. Maybe it is the sense of taste and memory that made me hold on to the last moments I had with him.

Being such a pronounced and impactful spice, cardamom has really made its mark in Oman and Zanzibar. The major influences in Omani cuisine came during the height of its maritime force, which began in the 17th century when Oman conquered the Portuguese-ruled Indian Ocean. Located on the southeast of the Arabian Peninsula, Oman was able to take the lead across the Arabian Sea and Indian Ocean while conquering a few of its neighbouring countries, such as southwest Iran, the coast of Balochistan and most of the Swahili coast, all the way down to Mozambique.

Oman's takeover had a key focus on the archipelago of Zanzibar due to its strategic geographical position and the abundance of cloves grown on the island, along with the trades in ivory and enslaved people. At the time, cloves were more valuable than gold. They were and remain today the island's biggest export. My paternal great-grandfather's livelihood was built off the back of having a clove farm, and cloves were so important to their family that when, in 1963, Babu's brother, Ali Hussain Darwish, was asked to design the flag that would represent Zanzibar after its independence from the British, he drew a pair of cloves.

However, the island was also known for having an abundance of cinnamon, nutmeg, vanilla, black pepper and, in particular, cardamom. This beloved spice of the people may be the underdog compared to the clove, but I would say it is found in at least 80 per cent of Zanzibari and Omani dishes. My grandmother always says that if something has too strong a smell of meat, flour or yeast, then you must add cardamom, while my mother believes that cardamom solves all the problems you may encounter with sweet dishes. I would say cardamom is to us what vanilla is to Western baking today. Although a cardamom pod has such a distinct flavour and smell, it's much more than an exotic, aromatic spice; it's a staple ingredient that transforms our dishes, making them deliciously and distinctively ours.

When I use cardamom, I think about the way that this single spice and flavour evokes a whole era of history, which we continue to remember through our food. One food in particular that tells this story is the *mandazi*, sometimes known as *mahamri* by the Kenyan *qabayel* (see page 22) in Oman. *Mandazis* are like French beignets, but made with cardamom and coconut, two of the most significant crops from Zanzibar.

Mandazi

Coconut & Cardamom Beignets

Makes 24

400ml (14fl oz) can of coconut
    milk, warmed
7g (scant ¼oz) fast-action dried
    yeast (1 packet)
650–700g (generous 5 cups) plain
    (all-purpose) flour, plus extra
    for dusting
200g (1 cup) caster (superfine)
    sugar
1 tbsp unsalted butter
1 tbsp ground cardamom or
    15 cardamom pods, crushed
1 litre (4⅓ cups) vegetable oil or
    sunflower oil, for deep-frying

Whenever someone in Oman finds out you have Zanzibari roots, the first thing they ask is if you can make *mandazi*. Growing up, my cousins would flock to these when a fresh batch was ready. I was the only one who wouldn't eat them, making my mother feel rather embarrassed to say I was her kid. Eventually, though, my taste buds kicked in, and I feel *mandazi* were what began my love affair with cardamom. You'll find them sold on the streets of Zanzibar and in the bakeries of Oman, always with coconut and always with cardamom – never let someone give you one without! – but I like our homemade ones the best. We always keep some dough tucked in the freezer ready to defrost on a Friday night and fry or bake on a Saturday morning. They are perfect for dunking in your tea, or filling with jam or chocolate spread. When there is no flatbread around for our curries, we even use these to mop up dinner. These pillowy, triangular clouds are versatile, comforting and moreish. Swahili legend has it that if the *mandazi* puff up when frying, it means the chef is hungry. So I recommend frying these on an empty stomach!

These are great on their own, but also delicious dusted with icing (confectioners') sugar. You could also try sprinkling them with sesame seeds before frying. Sometimes I even slip a piece of chocolate into the dough to melt as they cook!

Pour the warm coconut milk into a bowl. Add the yeast and leave to sit for 2 minutes.

Tip 650g (generous 5 cups) of the flour into a large bowl or a mixer, along with the sugar, butter and cardamom. Add the coconut and yeast mixture and knead for 25 minutes by hand or 15 minutes in the mixer. The dough should come together into a smooth ball with no excess flour; if it's too sticky, add another 50g (generous ⅓ cup) flour. Cover the bowl with cling film (plastic wrap) or a clean tea towel and leave to rest in a warm place for 1–2 hours until the dough has doubled in size.

Transfer the risen dough to a well-floured surface and separate into six pieces. Knead each piece slightly, then shape into a smooth ball.

Take the first ball and roll it out into a flat circle to a thickness of 1cm (½in). Using a knife or pizza cutter, cut it into quarters, leaving you with four triangles. Repeat with the other balls of dough. Cover the triangles with a clean cloth and leave to rise for another 30–45 minutes.

Recipe continues overleaf

Coasts

When you're ready to cook the *mandazi*, heat the oil in a large saucepan over a high heat. To test if the oil is hot enough, carefully drop a triangle into the oil. It should rise straight to the top and begin to puff up. If so, add a few more triangles, making sure you leave enough room in the pan for them to move around.

Cook for about 2–4 minutes until browned slightly on one side, then flip over to do the same on the other side. They say a true test of whether a *mandazi* is ready is it should look like it's about to pop, and should also have a white rim around the middle – so look out for those signs.

Make sure to keep an eye on the temperature of your oil; if the *mandazi* turn a dark brown very quickly, that's a sign to lower the heat. Once the first batch is cooked, transfer to a plate lined with kitchen paper (paper towels) to drain the excess oil while you fry the rest.

Serve the *mandazi* with your chosen accompaniments. These are best eaten straight away.

If you want to keep them overnight, store in an airtight container so they don't dry out and harden. They can also be frozen and reheated in a low oven.

Bahari Tonic

Serves 2

15g (½oz) basil leaves, plus extra
    to garnish
ice cubes
400–500ml (1¾–generous 2 cups)
    tonic water

**For the spiced simple syrup
(makes 100ml/scant ½ cup)**

12 cardamom pods
1 cinnamon stick
10 cloves
10 juniper berries
150g (1 cup plus 2 tbsp) caster
    (superfine) sugar

Oman has two mountains that are known for having the most magnificent juniper berry trees. Both Jebel Akdhar, which is in the Al Dahkhilya governorate, and the Hajar Mountains, the northernmost point in Oman, are surrounded by these majestic trees. The berries were once used for medicinal purposes, but now farmers have no use for them and simply don't know what to do with them, so the trees are monitored and looked after by flora and fauna experts.

In the UK, the flavour of juniper is most often associated with gin, but the berries themselves can be used in a simple spiced syrup as the base for a fragrant non-alcoholic fizz. Here, I've combined a few of our most beloved spices with fresh basil, to bring you a delightfully aromatic Bahari tonic. (According to my friend Kitty, though, adding a shot of gin to your glass will also bring you a gorgeous G&T.)

Begin by making your spiced simple syrup. Crush the cardamom pods using a pestle and mortar, then add to a small saucepan, along with the cinnamon, cloves, juniper berries, sugar and 150ml (⅔ cup) of water. Bring to the boil over a high heat, then continue to cook for exactly 10 minutes.

Remove from the heat and allow to cool completely. This syrup will keep in a sterilised glass jar for up to 2 weeks, either at room temperature or in the fridge.

To make the drinks, crush the basil leaves in the bottom of a cocktail shaker to break them down and release their flavour and aroma. Add 20ml (4 teaspoons) of the syrup along with some ice, and shake very well, then strain into two tumblers.

Add some fresh ice, then top up each glass with tonic water. Stir well and serve with a basil leaf to garnish.

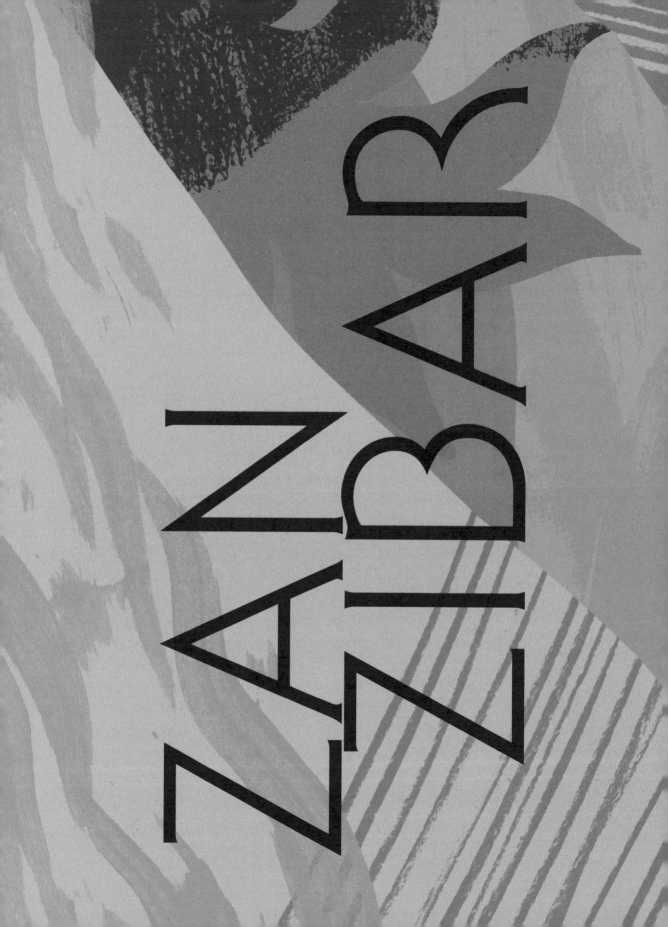

I should have just called this "the Bibi chapter". I think I learned almost all of these recipes – if not all of them – from my grandma. This chapter is everything she grew up with on the island of Zanzibar, and what she continues to cook today. When I watch Bibi make these dishes, I feel her sense of belonging. For her, it's a way to hold on to the country she had to leave, helping her to stay connected, no matter the distance. Most of what I have learned about Zanzibar has been through the stories Bibi shares with me as she cooks – every dish seems to summon up an evening or afternoon's worth of escapades she had on the island.

For the whole Zanzibari community in Portsmouth, these dishes have been at the crux of their shared identity, helping to make a new place feel like home. All the recipes are everyday comforts, things I love to whip up all the time, and I hope they will become the same for you.

Most Zanzibari recipes are cooked over fire or a hob, as ovens are not part of the island's culture. This lends a distinct, smoky aroma that is difficult to recreate in the kitchen, but possible nonetheless on a grill or a barbecue. As for ingredients, you'll notice a lot of coconut in this section; Zanzibaris have always been known as the coconut people. Wherever we can add it, we will.

Mchuzi wa Pweza

Zanzibari Coconut
Octopus Curry with
Pineapple & Physalis

Serves 6

1 small octopus, about 750g–1kg
(1lb 10oz–2¼lb)
1 tsp salt
1 tbsp garlic paste
1 tbsp ginger paste
400g (14oz) can chopped
tomatoes
1 onion, thinly sliced
1 red chilli, roughly chopped
1 tbsp baharat spice blend (see
page 120) or garam masala
2 tsp ground turmeric
600ml (2½ cups) coconut milk
200g (7oz) pineapple, peeled and
chopped into cubes
juice of 1 lemon
handful of coriander (cilantro),
finely chopped
100g (3½oz) physalis fruit, halved
(optional)

Since I was young, Bibi has tried her hardest to stop me from eating octopus. Besides not eating pork for religious reasons, she also avoids lobster, shark and, as she says, "anything little running around the sea". The first time I tried octopus was on my first trip to Zanzibar when I was 11. My mum hadn't been back since I was born, and we ended up running round the town like kids in a playground, eating everything she had missed and craved.

One evening, we passed by the Forodhani night market for a bite to eat. This spot is the place to bask in every Zanzibari dish; from sunset, the park billows with smoke from the countless barbecues lined up ready to grill freshly caught seafood. That night, I was enraptured by the Maasai men jumping high above my head as they entertained tourists, while my mum was drooling over the endless amounts of charred octopus tentacles ready to be eaten. We grabbed a platter of the Zanzibari equivalent of surf-and-turf, and although I had Bibi's voice in the back of my head, I finally got to savour and devour my first octopus.

This recipe is typical in Zanzibar. A great place to try this dish when visiting the island is at a local restaurant called Lukmaan. While we love our grilled octopus, we also enjoy it with coconut and lots of chilli. Instead of rice, we usually eat this with a dish called *mseto* – a type of porridge made with mung beans, rice and coconut. The pineapple and physalis are very much my addition; I find the flavours in this dish super rich, and the fruit really brings a delicate acidity to balance this.

Place your octopus in a saucepan with enough water to cover it, along with the salt and garlic and ginger pastes. Bring to the boil over a high heat and boil for 1 hour.

Meanwhile, in a large saucepan over a medium heat, combine the tomatoes, onion, chilli and ground spices. Stir in 400ml (1¾ cups) of the coconut milk and cook for 20 minutes, then reduce the heat to low and leave the sauce to simmer while the octopus continues to cook.

Once the octopus has finished boiling, remove it from the water and chop into small pieces. Stir these pieces into the sauce, along with the rest of your coconut milk, and leave to simmer for another 30 minutes.

Add the pineapple and leave to cook for another 20 minutes, then stir in the lemon juice and coriander. Taste for seasoning, and add more salt if needed. Cook for a final 10 minutes until the octopus is tender.

Garnish with the physalis and serve with your chosen accompaniments.

Kababu ya Samaki/Kabab Samak

Tuna Kebabs/Fishcakes

Makes 15–16 pieces

1 potato, peeled
5 tbsp vegetable oil, plus extra
    for deep-frying
2 red onions, roughly chopped
2 garlic cloves, peeled
500g (1lb 2oz) fresh tuna,
    cut into small cubes, or
    canned tuna, drained
1 tbsp ground cumin
1 tbsp freshly ground black
    pepper
1 tsp ground cinnamon
1 tsp ground cardamom
1 tsp ground turmeric
1 tsp salt
juice of ½ lemon
30g (1oz) coriander (cilantro)
1–2 green chillies
    (optional, if you like heat)
2 eggs
150g (5½oz) breadcrumbs

When Bibi moved to the UK in 1965, she didn't speak English, but adapting her cooking to suit the ingredients and equipment now available to her seemed to be a harder adjustment than learning another language. There were so many dishes and cooking methods she had to adapt; until she moved here, she had never even seen an oven! These fishcakes, kebabs or cutlets (whatever you might call them), known as *kababu ya samaki* in Swahili or *kabab samak* in Arabic, aren't necessarily unique or mind-blowing, but when Bibi first moved to the UK, they certainly were. She'd always made these back home with fresh tuna, but when she moved here, she was introduced to the canned version. The concept of fish in a can seems so normal to us, but for her it was obscene. Despite her reservations, she had a family to look after, so she took some home, worked with what she had and managed to recreate her Zanzibari fish kebabs. To this day, she still uses canned tuna to make them; she now considers it the greatest of inventions. If you have access to good-quality fresh tuna, though, I recommend using it. Tinned or fresh salmon also work beautifully.

Bring a saucepan of water to the boil. Add the potato and boil for 15 minutes until soft enough to mash. Drain and mash, then set aside.

Meanwhile, heat the 5 tablespoons of oil in a frying pan over a high heat. Add the onions and fry for 10–12 minutes until turning ever so slightly golden on the edges, then add the garlic cloves and sauté for 1 minute. Now stir in the tuna, followed by all the spices and salt. If you're using fresh tuna, fry for 10–15 minutes until the fish is cooked and all the liquid has evaporated. If you're using canned tuna, fry for a good 8–10 minutes until well combined.

Once the mixture is dry, add the lemon juice and mashed potato, then fry off for 5 minutes until dry.

Tip this mixture into a food processor. Add the coriander and chilli(es) and blitz until smooth. Taste for seasoning, adding some more salt and lemon if needed.

Using your hands, shape the mixture into 15–16 oblongs.

Pour oil into a large frying pan to a depth of 10cm (4in) for deep-frying and place over a high heat.

While the oil is heating up, beat the eggs in a bowl and scatter the breadcrumbs over a plate or shallow dish. Dip the fishcakes into the egg, then roll in the breadcrumbs to coat. Carefully transfer to the pan and fry on all sides for 3–4 minutes until golden and crisp.

Serve as a side dish or on their own. I love to serve these with my Chatini dip (see page 181).

Katles/Katlesi

Lamb Potato Cutlets/Chops

Makes 10

salt, to taste
1kg (2¼lb) potatoes, peeled
2 tsp black peppercorns
3 tsp cumin seeds
2 tsp coriander seeds
2 tbsp neutral oil, such as light
    vegetable oil, plus extra for
    deep-frying
1 red chilli, finely chopped
1 tsp garlic paste
2 onions, finely chopped
500g (1lb 2oz) minced lamb
20g (¾oz) coriander (cilantro),
    chopped
juice of ½ lemon
2 eggs

You might know these as potato chops, cutlets or croquettes; this is simply the way my family do them. Until I grew up, I never knew another way existed. Spiced, herby mince encased in fluffy mashed potato and then fried to seal: these are simple, comforting and carby, and easy to make for a family gathering or get-together. We eat them with a chilli sauce, my homemade Tamarind Sauce or my coconut Chatini (see page 181). If you like, you could use these spices and herbs and mix with vegetables such as okra, aubergine (eggplant)or peas.

Bring a large pan of salted water to the boil. Add the potatoes and boil for 20 minutes until they are soft and mashable.

Meanwhile, make the meat filling. Grind together the peppercorns and cumin and coriander seeds using a pestle and mortar.

Heat the 2 tablespoons of oil in a frying pan over a medium–high heat. Add the chilli, garlic paste and onions. Once they begin sizzling, sauté for 2 minutes. Add the mince and ground spices, and fry, stirring to break up the mince, for 15 minutes until brown and cooked through.

Once the meat is cooked, add the fresh coriander and lemon juice. Sauté for a further minute, then take off the heat and set aside to cool.

Drain your potatoes well and mash until smooth. Allow to cool.

To make your *katlesi*, take about 2 heaped tablespoons of the mashed potato and flatten it in your hand so it covers your palm. Place about ½ tablespoon of the meat filling in the middle of the potato, then wrap the rest of the potato around it. Roll the *katlesi* between both palms to smooth it out, then squish it slightly to make a cake-like shape. Repeat until all of the mashed potato and filling are used up.

Pour oil into a large frying pan over a high heat to a depth of 10cm (4in). Heat the oil until very hot. Meanwhile, crack the eggs into a bowl and beat well. To check if the oil is hot enough for frying, drop in a small dollop of whisked egg; if it cooks instantly, the oil is ready.

When you're ready to fry, dip the first *katlesi* into the egg to coat it fully, then carefully transfer to the hot oil. It should sizzle as it touches the oil. Cook for 4 minutes until golden on one side, then carefully flip and cook on the other side. Transfer to a plate lined with kitchen paper (paper towels) to drain the excess oil while you fry the rest. You can cook a few at a time, but take care not to overcrowd the pan.

Serve these on their own, or as a side dish or starter, with your chosen accompaniments.

Mchicha

Creamed Coconut Spinach

Serves 3–4

1 onion, thinly sliced
600g (1lb 5oz) spinach
400ml (14fl oz) can of coconut milk
1 red chilli, chopped
1 tsp ground turmeric
½ tsp salt, or to taste

Mchicha is the Swahili name for spinach. I never thought much of this recipe; we have it so often that it never seemed special. But I remember sharing it online, and the interaction and love for it was crazy. Who would have thought so many people loved creamed spinach? Adding coconut seemed to be a game-changer, and today this is still a recipe of mine that both followers and friends always speak about. If you are looking for a good, easy veggie side, this is the one. Great on toast, mopped up with flatbread or eaten with rice – or, if you're like my friend Kitty, then simply on its own. I also use this as the base to my Spinach and Coconut Shakshuka (see page 199).

Combine all the ingredients in a saucepan and place over a high heat. Cover with a lid and bring to the boil, then leave to boil for 10 minutes until the spinach has wilted.

At this stage, you'll have a very soupy coconut spinach. Remove the lid and leave to bubble and reduce for 15–20 minutes until most of the liquid has evaporated and you have a thick, creamy spinach. Serve with your chosen accompaniments.

Pilau

Zanzibari Cumin & Chicken Rice

Serves 4–5

120ml (½ cup) vegetable oil
1 onion, finely diced
3 tbsp cumin seeds
2 tbsp black peppercorns
2 cinnamon sticks
8 cardamom pods, crushed
6 cloves
2 tbsp garlic paste
4 medium or large potatoes,
   peeled and quartered
1 whole chicken, about 1.5kg
   (3lb 3oz), skin removed,
   cut into pieces (or use precut
   skinless pieces of your choice,
   on the bone)
1 tsp salt
350g (1¾ cups) basmati rice,
   rinsed
50g (1¾oz) raisins

I consider this dish a Zanzibari version of a Sunday roast. For my family, at least, it's always been a weekly dish that we make the time to gather at the table for. It's simple and easy to make, and only needs one pot, which is great. I would say this is the most recognisable and well-known dish from Zanzibar. It's usually made with chicken or lamb; I have also tried it with prawns, which works well if you don't eat meat. Whichever protein you choose, remember it is essential you serve it with my Kachumbar salad (see page 121) and a banana, a common custom across the Swahili coast when serving rice dishes, especially pilau.

Heat the oil in a large saucepan over a medium–high heat. Add the onion and sauté for 10 minutes until translucent, then stir in all the spices and the garlic paste and fry for another 2–3 minutes.

Next, add the potatoes and chicken. Fry for a further 8–10 minutes, stirring occasionally, then add 825ml (scant 1½ pints) of water and the salt. Bring to the boil and let it bubble for 20 minutes until the chicken is mostly cooked.

Rinse the rice well under running water, then tip it into the saucepan, along with the raisins. Wait for the water to come to the boil again, then reduce the heat to low. Securely wrap a clean tea towel around the lid of your pan to lock in the steam, then place on top and leave to cook for 30 minutes until the chicken, potatoes and rice are cooked through.

Plate up the rice on a large serving platter and serve with *kachumbar* and bananas.

Sambusa

Chicken Samosas

Makes 30–32

35g (¼ cup) plain (all-purpose) flour
about 60 samosa pastry sheets
1 litre (4⅓ cups) vegetable oil

For the filling

750g (1lb 10oz) chicken breasts or boneless chicken thighs
1 tsp salt
1 tsp freshly ground black pepper
2 tbsp garlic paste
1 tbsp vegetable oil
2 onions, finely chopped
1 tbsp baharat spice blend (see page 120) or garam masala
100ml (scant ½ cup) fresh lemon juice
100g (3½oz) coriander (cilantro), finely chopped
2 green chillies, finely chopped (optional)

Cooking notes:

These store well in the freezer; just prepare the samosas and freeze before frying. We tend to make a large batch ahead of Ramadan, then freeze them and fry each day!

If you can't find samosa pastry sheets, you can use spring roll pastry sheets, but you'll need to cut them to size.

These are delicious served with my Tamarind Sauce (see page 181).

There are thousands of chicken samosa recipes out there, but quite frankly, nothing beats our family's version. I always find the Omani-Zanzibari way of making samosas is so moreish and addictive. As a child, I had a habit of only eating the crunchy corners and then leaving the rest for someone else; nowadays, you won't even see a *crumb* left on my plate! This recipe would also work with minced meat and veg, but my favourite version is always chicken. Try your hardest to make these with samosa pastry, which you can find in most local Mediterranean and Asian shops. A little trick: for perfectly crunchy samosas, always fry from room-temperature oil. It's a game-changer, and will have them staying crunchy for longer!

To make the filling, combine the chicken, salt, black pepper and 1 tablespoon of the garlic paste in a saucepan over a medium heat. Add 250ml (1 cup plus 1 tbsp) of water and cook until the chicken is cooked through and the water has been absorbed; depending on the thickness of your chicken, this could take up to 45 minutes.

Once the chicken is cooked, use two forks to shred it in the pan until you have thin strands. Set aside.

Heat 1 tablespoon of the oil in a frying pan over a medium heat. Add the onions and fry for 10 minutes until translucent, then add the remaining garlic paste and stir through. Cook for 2 minutes, then add the baharat or garam masala. Stir well to combine, then fry for a further 2 minutes.

Next, add the shredded chicken, lemon juice, coriander and chillies (if using) and stir through until everything is mixed and distributed evenly. Take off the heat and leave to cool slightly before assembling the samosas.

To make the paste for sealing the samosas, mix the flour with 50ml (scant ¼ cup) of water in a small bowl or cup until you have a mixture thick enough to act like glue.

Recipe continues overleaf

Zanzibar

To fold the samosas, take a samosa pastry strip and position it with one of the short ends towards you. Place 1 heaped tablespoon of the chicken mixture at the bottom, in the middle, then pick up the bottom right-hand corner and fold it over the filling to line up with the left-hand edge of the pastry. It will look roughly like a right-angled triangle.

While holding that down, grab the bottom left-hand corner and tightly pull it over to the right, again lining it up with the edge of the pastry. At this point, you will have closed up the gaps and have the beginnings of a triangle.

Keep folding from right to left until you reach the top, and then dab a little bit of the flour paste on the inside of the pastry to seal.

Wrap a second sheet of pastry around the samosa following the same method to give it a second layer, then set aside and repeat with the remaining filling and pastry strips.

When you're ready to fry your samosas, pour the oil into a large saucepan. You'll need to fry the samosas in batches of about a third at a time. Place the first batch into the oil at room temperature, then turn the heat to high. The samosas will cook as the oil heats up; this will take about 10 minutes. Once the oil is hot, continue to cook the samosas for about 4 minutes on each side. You will see them begin to change colour; once they are golden/deep brown, remove from the oil with a slotted spoon and place on a plate lined with kitchen paper (paper towels) to drain the excess oil.

For the next batches, if you can wait and let the oil cool back to room temperature before you begin, that will always work best. But if not, cook the remaining batches for 2–3 minutes on each side, and make sure the ones cooked in hot oil are eaten first, as the first batch will stay crunchier for longer.

ZANZIBARI STREET FOOD

Back in the early 1940s, Bibi and her big brother Gigi would visit Forodhani, a garden in the heart of Zanzibar's capital, Stone Town. They would head there with their father for a weekly treat. Most of the town headed to the same spot, all for the one and only Habib, an elderly Zanzibari man who sold ice cream, a sweet cardamom and rose milk known as *sherbati* in Swahili (see page 195 for my version), and native tropical fruits. Gigi always tells me he remembers Tuesday afternoons being a special day to visit Habib, as they would sit with their *sherbati* and ice cream while they watched the police band perform. Now, this same place has been transformed into a celebration of Zanzibar's street-food culture, and both tourists and locals flock there every night.

I was 11 when I first visited Zanzibar, and one of the strongest memories I have of that trip is Forodhani. The place seemed like a theme park for food. Never had I seen so much enthusiasm and entertainment around a barbecue; it made trips to Camden Town and Brick Lane look like a calm, quiet day out. The vigour and spirit that flowed through the atmosphere, from the beach through to the park, was like nothing else. Wherever you turned, there was someone trying to hustle you into tasting the food they had to offer, or beguiling Maasai groups busking for you. As kids we were taught to ask them to *ruka* (Swahili for "jump") as their traditional dance involves jumping, and the second they did, we would run for the ocean, wailing as we watched their extraordinary bounce take

them high above our 4ft-something heights! Not much has changed at the gardens. These days, I certainly don't challenge the Maasai to jump, but I do enjoy their flirtatious Swahili charisma now and then.

Now, as an adult among all the chaos, I notice the groups of locals engulfed in the day's gossip. Zanzibaris will unapologetically join you for a natter, teaching you about their spices, their history and how they make their own beer, as well as letting you in on the hidden gems of the island, at the same time as finding out about your whole life history! Depending on the day or season, you might also be lucky enough to catch live music

Above *Bibi with her children and cousins in Zanzibar in 1963;* **right** *Babu in his canning workshop in 1956;* **below, far left** *Bibi and Babu with friends and family in 1955.*

and festivals magnifying the already colossal atmosphere. During the day, the garden is a tranquil space to soak up the island breeze and listen to the waves as they crash against the shore. You'll find the odd vendor feeding the peckish and curious wanderers, but it's from sunset that the place transforms into a haze of smoke, filled with bustling, excited people ready to swoon over freshly caught seafood that's been charred on the grills, pick 'n' mix lemon-and-turmeric soup bowls and Zanzibar's famous pizza. All along the beachfront, Zanzibaris, mainlanders, and Syrian and Indian locals are just some of the multicultural islanders firing up flames, sizzling up pans and whipping up batters in preparation for an evening filled with bartering and business. The whole park is filled with rows of vendors showcasing tables full of various meats and vegetables on skewers, known as *mishkaki* in Swahili or *mishkak* in Arabic. Sometimes, if you are lucky, they may be serving venison, which was a very popular meat my grandfather would hunt for back in the day. You'll discover the best of the *bahari* (ocean), from squid to jumbo prawns, as well as my absolute favourite: the tenderest and tastiest octopus you'll ever have.

The most popular and best-known dish to have at the market is the "Zanzibar mix", a potato and lemon broth traditionally called *mbatata za urojo* (see page 168 for my version). With little to no spicing, the starch from the potatoes combines with lemon, tamarind and chilli to create sharp, eclectic, and buoyant flavours with every spoonful. Depending on the vendor, you'll have an array of meat and vegan toppings to choose from.

Zanzibar

167

Mbatata za Urojo (Zanzibar Mix)

Zanzibari Turmeric, Lemon, Potato & Chickpea Broth

Serves 4

2 tbsp olive oil
2 tbsp plain (all-purpose) flour
1 tsp garlic powder (optional)
1 tbsp ground turmeric
2 whole red chillies
salt, to taste
4 potatoes, peeled and chopped into 6–8 pieces
400g (14oz) can of chickpeas
juice of 1–2 lemons
1 tbsp tamarind paste (optional)

Optional garnishes
cornflakes
salt-and-vinegar crisps
sev or Bombay mix

Growing up, my cousins and I would call this recipe "yellow potatoes"; none of us could pronounce the Swahili name, and back then, we wanted it to sound "normal". This has to be our most famous street-food meal in Zanzibar. It's a very simple recipe, yet elite within the community. To help tourists, it's now known as "Zanzibar mix". The concept behind this soup is that you layer it according to your cravings. So you start with your base of potato soup, then choose from a selection of Zanzibari snacks to include in it, such as *bajiyas* (mung bean falafels), meat skewers, *kachori* (potato balls), tamarind water or paste, chilli sauce, coconut and coriander chutney and, to top it off, shredded cassava crisps. I add every single element possible, dropping them in and mixing it around before slurping away.

Making all these extra parts can be time consuming, though; my mum tells me that when she worked for the Royal Oman Police, she and her cousin Suki would round up their friends every week and they'd all bring in one element. They'd set up shop in the office as soon as they arrived at 7am, and have this for their breakfast. Since she moved to England, she's continued the same concept, getting all the women in the family to prepare a part for our gatherings, and creating our own food stall inside the house.

I make this constantly, especially in the winter, as it's so easy and comforting. I got into the habit of adding chickpeas, just to give it an extra dimension. While I don't always have the extra elements at my disposal, I do mimic the crunchy cassava by sprinkling over some Bombay mix or a mixture of cornflakes with salt-and-vinegar crisps!

In a large saucepan, combine the oil, flour, garlic powder and turmeric over a medium heat, whisking together to form a paste. Slowly pour in about 200ml (scant 1 cup) of water, whisking as you go to stop any lumps from forming.

Increase the heat to high, then pour in another 800ml (3¾ cups) of water, followed by the chillies. Season with salt and bring to the boil.

Once it's bubbling, add the potatoes. If your water looks red, add a dash of lemon – the turmeric needs acidity to stay yellow. Leave the potatoes to cook for 15–20 minutes, then add the chickpeas. The water should just cover the potatoes; you don't want too much, as it will take a lot longer to thicken.

Cook for a further 10 minutes, then add the lemon juice and taste for seasoning, adding more salt if needed. At this point, you can add the tamarind paste, if you like. If not, you can add some extra lemon if you want it more acidic. For me, the more lemon, the better!

Sprinkle on your chosen garnishes and serve.

Kachori

Deep-fried Potato Balls

Makes 15–16

540g (1lb 3oz) potatoes, peeled
   and quartered
salt, to taste
1 red chilli, finely chopped
½ tsp chilli powder
½ tsp garlic powder
1 tsp ground turmeric
25g (scant 1oz) coriander
   (cilantro), finely chopped
juice of 1 small lemon
vegetable oil, for frying

For the batter
100g (generous ¾ cup) gram flour
2 tsp salt
½ tsp chilli powder

If you needed one more reason to love potatoes, then this recipe is it. A very typical Zanzibari snack, these potato balls are also found in Oman. They're deep-fried, soft in the middle, and taste lemony and herby, with a kick of heat. I feel like these are the perfect marriage of my British and Zanzibari tastes: Brits love potatoes and find a million ways to use them, while Zanzibaris love frying their food and adding lemon to everything! Serve these with my Tamarind Sauce or coconut Chatini (see page 181).

Bring the potatoes to the boil in a saucepan of salted water over a high heat. Boil for 20 minutes, or until they are soft enough to mash.

Drain well, then return to the pan. Add the red chilli, chilli powder, garlic powder, turmeric and coriander. Season with salt and begin to mash.

Add the lemon juice slowly, a little at a time, mashing between each addition. You may not need all the lemon juice; you don't want it to make the potatoes too wet.

Once the mixture is well mashed, take pieces of the mixture and roll them into golf-ball-sized balls. Place all the balls in the fridge to chill for about 30 minutes.

Make the batter by mixing the gram flour, salt and chilli powder with 80ml (generous 5 tbsp) of water. Depending on your gram flour brand, you might need slightly more water. We don't want a thick batter; just enough to coat the balls.

When you're ready to fry the potato balls, pour oil into a saucepan to a depth of 10cm (4in) and place over a high heat.

Meanwhile, roll the *kachori* in the batter.

To check if the oil is hot enough for frying, drop in a small dollop of batter. If it rises straight away and starts sizzling, then the oil is ready. Working in batches so as not to overcrowd the pan, carefully drop the *kachori* into the saucepan and fry for a couple of minutes until slightly golden. Transfer to a plate lined with kitchen paper (paper towels) to drain the excess oil while you fry the rest.

Serve warm or at room temperature with your chosen accompaniments.

Mhogo Chips

Cassava Fries

Serves 2–3

2 fresh cassavas,
    about 650g (1lb 7oz)
1 litre (4⅓ cups) vegetable oil,
    for deep-frying
2 tbsp sumac
1–2 tsp chilli powder
salt, to taste

This is basically a Zanzibari version of chips or French fries. Cassava, like potato, is something we love in every shape and form. We grill it, boil it with meat or plantain, mash it and, of course, deep-fry it. Nowadays, you can buy precut cassava chips in supermarkets in the UK, which is totally awesome, but these are just as easy to make using fresh cassava, and the result is even tastier! Every street-food vendor in Zanzibar will serve these up with salt and chilli powder; it's pretty much our standard flavouring for everything. The sprinklings are totally up to you; whatever you prefer on your chips, feel free to add it and enjoy!

Peel and cut your cassavas into chips about 1–2.5cm (½–1in) thick and 7.5cm (3in) long. As you work, keep the sliced chips submerged in a bowl of cold water to stop them from browning.

Bring a pan of water to the boil over a high heat and add the cassava chips. Boil for exactly 5 minutes to give them a fluffy texture on the inside, then drain the chips and pat dry with kitchen paper (paper towel).

Pour the oil into a large saucepan over a high heat. You want the oil to be hot enough that when you add a piece of cassava, it sizzles. Test it out; once you get that sizzle, add the rest of the cassava. Fry for 10 minutes until golden brown, then transfer to a plate lined with kitchen paper to drain the excess oil.

While the chips are still warm, sprinkle over the sumac and chilli powder, then season with salt and toss well to coat them all before serving.

Coconut Turmeric Sweetcorn

You may have gathered by now that coconut and turmeric play a huge role in the Zanzibari side of my cooking. This dish is a simple elevation of boiled corn, and something we commonly have as a side dish at the dinner table. It makes for a wonderful snack, too!

I prefer to use coconut cream or coconut milk powder for this to keep it thick, but you can use canned coconut milk; just drain the coconut water from the can, so that the sauce takes less time to thicken.

Serves 4

8 half corn cobs
1 onion, diced
1 tbsp ground turmeric
½ tsp salt, or to taste
185g (6½oz) coconut cream
juice of ½ lemon
2 green chillies, halved (optional)

Combine the corn, onion and turmeric in a large saucepan with 1 litre (4⅓ cups) of water. Season with salt and bring to the boil over a high heat. Boil, uncovered, for about 15 minutes until the corn is cooked.

Add the coconut cream and stir well to combine, then leave to cook on a medium–high heat for 15–20 minutes until the liquid thickens.

Add the lemon juice and chillies (if using) and simmer for a further 5 minutes, then serve hot as a side dish.

IRAN & ZANZIBAR

My mother's parents have always been very proud to tell everyone they have Persian heritage. Historically in Zanzibar, being of a non-indigenous ethnic background, and especially of a lighter-skinned race (whether that was Arab, European or Persian), represented privilege and suggested a more aristocratic demeanour. Bibi in particular has always found it difficult to relate to or accept her African lineage on her father's side. Among some communities in Oman, being of Swahili background was always looked down on, so to fit in, Bibi placed an emphasis on her father's Iranian side and her mother's Omani side.

During the time of the revolution in Zanzibar, many of my grandfather's family fled to Iran. They were able to speak Farsi, and this migration gave them a chance to be closer to a heritage they had always been proud of. Although my grandparents eventually came to England, not a day has gone by that they didn't talk about that side of our family, the food or the country.

Iran's prominent connection with Zanzibar reaches back to the 13th century, long before Oman became involved with the south of Iran. However, before this – since the first century CE – Persian merchants would sail across the Indian Ocean during the monsoon winds to buy gold and silver. From the 1200s–1500s, trade between East Africa and the Persian Gulf grew strongly. Originally, merchants would travel to Mogadishu, the capital of Somalia; back then, it was the most important city to trade with along the coast. Merchants from Shiraz in Iran, the majority of whom travelled to East Africa, were known as the Shirazis. After establishing a base in Somalia, they began to migrate south of the Swahili coast, focusing on all the islands, from Lamu to Mafia, Pemba, Zanzibar, Kilwa and the Comoros. By the end of the 1200s, they had formed their own dynasty in East Africa, and continued to grow, dominating the northwest of the Indian Ocean by the 1500s.

*Left Babu in Tehran, 1975; **above** Babu's extended Iranian family.*

By the 16th century, the Portuguese had begun to take over, and eventually the Shirazi dynasty was no more. However, they continued to live and flourish in all the countries they had been involved with. Bibi recalls growing up with the whole community in Zanzibar. It wasn't until the revolution of 1964 that the Afro-Shirazi party came about – a party formed by African Iranians, who came together to fight against the Omanis, overthrow the Sultan and gain power once again.

Among the Shirazis there were pockets of other merchant families, such as Bibi's and Babu's. Bibi's paternal grandfather, Abdul Hussein Lare, was born in Bandar Abbas into a Lare (pronounced "Lari") *qabeela* who originated from Larestan, a county in the Fars province of south Iran. Bandar Abbas today is heavily influenced by Black Africans and is known for being home to many Afro-Iranians. With a port leading directly out onto the Gulf of Oman and down to the Indian Ocean, it was a prime location for merchants and was the first port of access to Iran for people from East Africa. While that side of the family chose the ocean route, Babu's grandfather chose to weave his way through the lands and sea before crossing to Zanzibar. His name was Darweish, which means "merchant" in Farsi. According to my mum's family tree discovery, he was born in the 1800s to a family who came from Shushtar, a southwestern county of Iran in the province of Khuzestan, which is very close to the Iraq border. Darweish had families everywhere, which means I have lots of long-lost relatives I hope to find one day. He had a family in Kuwait, then another one in Shushtar, before migrating to Oman, where he settled in a coastal town called Liwa, located in the Al-Batinah governorate. Here, he bred bees and became known as Darweish Asaal (*asaal* meaning "honey" in Arabic). He produced a decadent honey that he supplied to the palace in Sohar (the largest city in Al-Batinah), which brought him the privilege to be able to wear a Royal Bisht, an honour bestowed by the Sultan. After establishing a family and business in Oman, Darweish Asaal travelled to Saudi Arabia to a governorate called Al-Ahsa, where he met his last wife, Aliya (nicknamed Bi-Aliyoo by my family). From there, he decided to move to Zanzibar and live the rest of his life, where he swapped honey for clove farms, ultimately producing what my family believes to have been half of Zanzibar's clove exports, and so setting up my great-grandfather's future.

While I am yet to discover Iran, I have lived vicariously through the stories shared by my mother's family. They have always described the country and people in such an opulent way; they drool over the food and are forever nostalgic about their brief time living in and visiting Iran. Like Bibi, I love to tell people I have those roots, although they are roots I am still learning about; so I use the understanding I do have of them to create food that represents that side of my heritage.

Left Babu as a little
boy (pictured right);
above Bi-Aliyoo, my
Babu's grandmother.

Left Bibi with my mum and her sister in
Zanzibar, 1963; *above* Umukheir, Bibi's mother
and my great-grandmother; *far left* Umukheir
cooking pilau in Zanzibar in the 1980s.

Spinach, Lamb, Dried Lime & Pigeon Pea Stew

Serves 5–6

100ml (scant ½ cup) neutral oil, such as light vegetable oil, plus extra if needed

1 onion, thinly sliced

1 tbsp baharat spice blend (see page 120)

1–2 tsp salt

2 green chillies, finely chopped

1 tbsp garlic paste

1.5kg (3lb 3oz) fresh spinach

30g (1oz) coriander (cilantro), finely chopped

3 dried limes, pierced with a knife

500g (1lb 2oz) lamb shoulder or leg (no bones), chopped into 5cm (2in) pieces

400g (14oz) can of pigeon peas

This is a nostalgic recipe for my grandmother Bibi, who learned it in Zanzibar from her Iranian in-laws; it's based upon the Persian dish *ghormeh sabzi* (herb stew). They had to adapt it slightly to suit the ingredients that were available to them on the island; however, as the amazing women they were, they made it work. While the traditional version is made with fenugreek leaves and kidney beans, ours made use of spinach and pigeon peas. The same principles were applied to the dish, though, and to be honest, they taste almost the same. The addition of dried limes makes this delicious to eat the next day when the flavours have had the chance to infuse, so I always make sure to keep leftovers! Serve this up with chapatis (see page 182), white rice or saffron rice, and a yogurt-based salad.

Heat the oil in a large saucepan over a low–medium heat. Add the onion and fry for around 15 minutes until softened but not brown. Now add the baharat, salt, chillies, garlic paste, spinach and coriander, and fry until the spinach has wilted (you might need to add the spinach in batches so it can wilt down a little between additions to make space). Now, Bibi says you need to keep frying until the spinach releases a strong, aromatic smell. This takes at least 10–15 minutes, so make sure you have some oil on hand in case it dries up.

Next, add the dried limes, followed by the lamb. Fry off the lamb for 10 minutes until slightly browned, then pour in 1 litre (4⅓ cups) of water, making sure the lamb is completely covered. Cover with the lid and bring to the boil, then leave to bubble away over a medium–high heat for 30 minutes. Remove the lid and cook for another 30 minutes until the lamb is cooked through and the liquid has reduced.

Stir in the peas and cook for a further 25 minutes. The stew is now ready to serve, but if you take it off the heat and leave it to sit for a while before you eat, the dried lime has more time to work its magic.

Cooking notes:

You can make this with frozen spinach if you prefer.

This also works nicely as a vegetarian dish; leave out the lamb and add extra vegetables of your choice, such as sweet potatoes and courgettes (zucchini).

You can use kidney beans or pigeon peas.

Dill & Kidney Bean Rice

This recipe is based on the Iranian dish *sabzi polo* (herb rice), another recipe that Bibi was introduced to by her Iranian in-laws. While the traditional recipe uses various herbs, we have always made it with lots of dill. The addition of kidney beans came from Bibi, who was always trying to use up whatever she could find in the house, and it just stuck.

Serves 4–5

2 tbsp olive oil or vegetable oil
1 onion, finely chopped
15g (½oz) dried dill
15g (½oz) fresh dill, finely chopped
400g (2 cups) basmati rice
400g (14oz) can of kidney beans
salt, to taste

Heat the oil in a saucepan over a medium–high heat. Add the onion and fry for 8–10 minutes until translucent, then add the dried and fresh dill and fry for another 5 minutes. You may need to add a bit more oil if it clumps together.

Now stir in the rest of the ingredients, along with 800ml (3½ cups) of water. Season with salt to taste and mix well. Bring to the boil, then reduce the heat to low. Securely wrap a clean tea towel around the lid of the pan and place it on top to lock in the steam, then cook for 20–25 minutes until the rice is cooked through and fluffy. Serve.

Chatini

Coconut & Coriander Dip

Serves 6

150g (5oz) desiccated (dried, shredded) coconut – make sure it's not sweet
20g (¾oz) mint leaves
40g (scant 1½oz) fresh coriander
salt, to taste
zest and juice of 1 lemon

This is a go-to dip for Zanzibaris. We more or less have it with everything, and it takes just minutes to whip up. It's super tangy and usually very spicy, but you can reduce the heat if you wish. We also add dollops of this to our turmeric and potato soup (see my Mbatata za Urojo, page 168). It's best to use a bullet-type blender for this, to make sure the result is smooth enough.

Add everything to a blender with 400ml (1¾ cups) of water and blitz until really smooth. You will probably need to blend it for at least 1 minute, as the desiccated coconut takes a while to break down. You want to make sure it is super-smooth and not too grainy from the coconut.

Serve right away, or chill and serve cold. This will keep for about 4 days in the fridge, but you may need to loosen it with a little water before serving as it will thicken when chilled.

Tamarind Sauce

Serves 10

50g (1¾oz) tamarind block
2 tbsp tomato ketchup
30g (1oz) coriander (cilantro)
2–3 hot green chillies
salt, to taste

A holy grail sauce for Omanis and Zanzibaris: whether we're adding it to our soups or dipping our meat skewers in it, there is always tamarind sauce available. We like it tangy and spicy – if it's not those two things, it's not for us.

Before you begin, soak the tamarind in 400ml (1¾ cups) of water in a bowl for at least 30 minutes to soften.

Using your hands, squeeze the tamarind in the water to turn it into pulp, then strain through a sieve to remove the seeds.

Add the tamarind pulp and soaking water to a blender, along with the rest of the ingredients, and blitz until smooth.

Store in an airtight container in the fridge for up to 5 days.

Mkate wa Kusukuma

Coconut Chapati

**Makes 10 large chapatis or
20 small ones**

710g (5½ cups) plain (all-purpose)
   flour, plus extra for dusting
3–4 tsp salt
500ml (generous 2 cups)
   coconut milk
about 250g (9oz) warm ghee

Chapati to us is like paratha to everyone else, as we make our chapati with lots of layers. However, we also use coconut milk instead of water. This is common in Zanzibar, where coconut milk is cleaner and cheaper than water, and comes in abundance. Bibi and my mum also taught me that using coconut milk in your bread makes it stay softer for longer, so it has become a habit for me to use it in dough recipes.

I used to find these chapatis so tedious and hard to make, but now I find it quite therapeutic. Some of my followers have told me it makes for a great children's activity, keeping them busy with all that folding and rolling. Our way of creating the layers brings you so many, making these chapatis extra flaky. They freeze perfectly, too, so you can spend a day making a batch, then freeze them for up to a month and fry whenever you fancy one. Serve with a lush, thick stew, or enjoy drizzled with honey – or simply on their own.

In a large bowl or mixer, combine your flour, salt and coconut milk with 4 tablespoons of the ghee. Knead for 15–18 minutes by hand, or for 10 minutes if using a mixer, until the mixture comes together into a smooth dough. Once it is smooth, knead the dough into a soft ball. Cover with a clean, damp cloth and leave to rest for at least 10 minutes and up to 30 minutes.

Once rested, evenly divide the dough into 10 or 20 balls (depending on how many chapatis you want). Cover the balls with a damp cloth while you work.

Take one ball and start rolling it out on a floured work surface. You want to roll it out until it's super thin, so that you can almost see through it. You'll probably notice that as you roll, it will start to spring back. If this happens, take a dribble of ghee and spread it on the work surface, then take some more and wipe it on the dough. This will help the dough to stretch. You may find that using your hands to stretch the dough is easier. Don't worry if the dough rips a little bit, but don't allow the whole thing to become covered in holes!

Once you have stretched out the dough as thinly as possible, dribble a couple of teaspoons of ghee over it, then use your hands to wipe it all over. The aim is to make sure that the dough is not dry, but you don't want it soggy and dripping either, so add slowly.

Now poke a hole in the middle of the dough and, using both your hands, start "rolling" the hole outwards until you have created one giant ring of dough. Create a break in the ring and form a long sausage shape. If it looks slightly loose from the rolling, just roll it between your hands to neaten it up slightly.

Recipe continues overleaf

Now it's time for the final layering. You will need to form a spiral at each end of the sausage – at the same time! – so you end up with two spirals that meet in the middle.

Once they meet, fold one on top of the other and press down slightly so they stick. Place back under the cloth and repeat with the rest of the dough (it gets easier!).

Once all the chapatis are ready, leave to rest for at least 20 minutes at room temperature, or overnight in the fridge. At this point, you can also freeze them to fry another day.

When you're ready to cook, take the first piece of spiralled dough and roll it out until it's about 5mm (¼in) thick. Place it in a dry non-stick frying pan over a high heat.

Fry for 2 minutes until the bottom of the chapati starts to cook and firm up. Flip over and spread some ghee all over (no dry bits!). Cook for a couple of minutes until firm, then flip again. Spread this side with ghee and cook for a further couple of minutes until cooked on both sides. The chapati should be cooked through with cute brown streaks, and may even puff up (always a good sign – if this happens, just take your spatula and press it down).

Once it's ready, transfer to a plate and cover with foil to keep warm while you fry the rest. Serve with your chosen accompaniments (see page 178), or just on their own!

Tips:

These chapatis are best enjoyed right away, but will keep, wrapped in cling film (plastic wrap) in the fridge, for up to a week.

They can also be frozen for up to a month and reheated in a frying pan with some ghee.

Zanzibar

Chila

Coconut Rice Pancakes

Makes 9–10

200g (1 cup) basmati rice
7g (scant ¼ oz) fast-action
    dried yeast (1 packet)
200ml (scant 1 cup) warm
    coconut milk
110g (generous ½ cup) caster
    (superfine) sugar
8 cardamom pods, ground
salted or unsalted butter, for
    frying (use plant-based butter
    to make this vegan)

Chila are Zanzibari pancakes made from rice and coconut milk, lightly scented with cardamom. They are gluten-free and can be vegan. I've always grown up having these as an all-day food; I've watched Mum roll them up and dunk them in her morning cup of tea, but I've also enjoyed them as a midday snack or placed them on the dinner table ready to enjoy after our main course. I use similar ingredients to make the batter for my Mkate wa Kumina (see page 140), but the method is slightly different. When I make these, I love to play around with the toppings. I mostly enjoy them with fruits and chocolate, but once in a while, I'll have them with savoury dishes, such as lentil or chickpea curries and fried chicken! Please note the rice needs to be soaked for at least 2–3 hours or ideally overnight, and you'll also need a high-powered blender.

Soak the rice in a bowl of water overnight, or for at least 2–3 hours, then drain.

In a separate bowl, add the yeast to the coconut milk and leave to bloom for 5 minutes, then pour into a high-powered blender, along with the drained rice, sugar and cardamom. Blend everything together until the rice has completely broken down and is no longer grainy. You want the smoothest texture possible.

Pour the mixture into a large bowl and cover with cling film (plastic wrap), then leave in a warm area to rise for about 30 minutes–1 hour until the mixture has doubled in size and has bubbles on the top.

When you're ready to cook, place a non-stick frying pan over a medium heat and add a little butter. Using a ladle, scoop some batter from the bowl and pour into the frying pan to create a circle about 12.5cm (5in) in diameter (if you like, you can make them a different size – it depends how big you like your pancakes). Repeat with more batter, depending on the size of your pan, then reduce the heat to low. Cover the pan with a lid so that the pancakes steam and don't dry out – you want them to retain their moisture.

Let the pancakes cook slowly for 3–4 minutes. Do not flip them! You will notice little holes forming on the top as the batter begins to cook. Once they are cooked through and completely dry on top, remove from the pan and transfer to a plate while you make the rest.

Serve cold or warm with your chosen accompaniments. These can be frozen once cooked.

Plantain or Banana, Coconut & Cardamom Cake

Serves 6–8

160g (5¾oz) plantain or banana, puréed, plus 1 sliced
200g (generous 1½ cups) plain (all-purpose) flour
2 tsp baking powder
80g (6½ tbsp) caster (superfine) sugar
80g (6½ tbsp) soft light brown sugar
100g (3½oz) desiccated (dried, shredded) coconut
3 eggs
185ml (generous ¾ cup) vegetable oil
10 cardamom pods, crushed, or 1 tbsp ground cardamom

For the caramel
100g (½ cup) soft light brown sugar
3 tbsp unsalted butter

Ever since I was little, Bibi and my mum have been adamant that I had to enjoy *all* of our home cooking, but until I was about 16, I refused to eat any dishes that looked too "different", and especially avoided anything with an overwhelming taste of cardamom. I couldn't stand the spice, which was really unhelpful, because almost every single recipe of ours included it. There is one particular pudding from Zanzibar called *ndizi mbivu*, which is basically overripe sweet plantains stewed with coconut milk and cardamom. As a kid, the look of the dish always put me off – it looked messy, unlike all the pretty, quintessentially British puddings I was used to seeing. Much to Bibi's dismay, I would compare it to baby food and always turn up my nose at it. I must have been about 20 when I started to appreciate it and understand how something so simple could yield so much comfort and flavour.

Now, I see the warmth of the cardamom and the creaminess of the coconut is bliss, and I've included my version on page 141. However, I also wanted to include this "prettier" version: the version that let me feel as if I fitted in, and as if our food made sense. Bringing all the same ingredients into a cake seemed like the perfect way for others to relate to how comforting *ndizi mbivu* is for us. Even my mum and Bibi enjoy this version with a cup of tea.

Preheat the oven to 200°C (180°C fan/400°F/Gas 6). Grease a 20cm (8in) cake tin and line with baking parchment (parchment paper).

To make the caramel, place the sugar in a saucepan over a low–medium heat and allow it to gradually melt, gently swirling the pan to help ensure all the sugar melts evenly. Once it has all melted, add the butter and keep stirring until smooth.

Arrange the sliced banana or plantain in the base of the prepared tin, then pour over the caramel. Set aside.

Combine all the remaining ingredients together in a large bowl and whisk until fully incorporated and smooth, but don't over-whisk. Pour the batter into the tin over the sliced banana or plantain and caramel. Bake for 20 minutes, then reduce the oven temperature to 190°C (170°C fan/375°F/Gas 5) and bake for a further 25 minutes until a skewer inserted into the middle comes out clean.

Leave to cool in the tin for about 10 minutes, then remove from the tin. I like to serve this warm, but if you prefer you can leave it to cool entirely – just be sure to remove from the tin while it's still warm. This will keep for 4–5 days in an airtight container.

Pompia

Rhubarb & Geranium Sorbet

Serves 4–5

500g (1lb 2oz) rhubarb
  (as red/pink as possible),
  chopped into 5cm (2in) chunks
175g (¾ cup plus 2 tbsp) caster
  (superfine) sugar
15g (½oz) rose geranium leaves,
  or 2 tbsp dried lavender petals

Bibi's mum – also known as Bibi Wa Kati, meaning "the middle *bibi*", as she was the middle of her siblings – always used to make her own scented oil for soothing aches and pains and nourishing hair. It was made with coconut, pepper, turmeric and a few essential oils, including geranium. During the Covid-19 lockdown, Bibi decided she wanted to start making some herself. She swears it helps her arthritis and any pains we get. I use it often and always feel fabulous after.

While Bibi was making her oils, I was taking a cooking course run by Ravneet Gill and Nicola Lamb called the PUFF Pastry School, which helped me build the foundations of baking and pastry skills. One of the weeks was dedicated to sorbets, and I decided that since we had loads of scented geranium growing in my mum's front garden, I would try using it in a sorbet. After it had been churned, my mum and I sat down to enjoy it, and it was truly beautiful. I have been obsessed with this sorbet ever since! I like to think my great-grandmother would have loved it, too.

Ask your neighbours, family and friends if they have any scented geraniums in their garden. The bushes grow really big, so they wouldn't miss a few leaves if you cut some off. Do not use geranium oil, as it is not food-safe. If you can't find scented geranium leaves, dried lavender or rose petals will bring the same harmonious joy to this sorbet.

Place the rhubarb in a bowl with 25g (2 tbsp) of the sugar. Add 5 teaspoons of water and stir to combine, then leave to macerate for 20–30 minutes.

Meanwhile, put the geranium leaves into a small saucepan with 200ml (scant 1 cup) of water. Place over a high heat. Once it begins to bubble, boil for exactly 2 minutes, then add the remaining sugar. Give it a good stir, then leave on a vigorous boil for another 5 minutes until the sugar has dissolved. Remove from the heat and leave to cool completely.

Preheat the oven to 210°C (190°C fan/410°F/Gas 6½) and line a roasting tray with baking parchment (parchment paper).

Once the rhubarb has macerated, tip it on to the prepared tray and spread out into a single layer. Roast for 15 minutes, then leave to cool.

Strain the sugar syrup through a sieve into a jug, making sure you squeeze the geranium leaves to extract as much flavour as possible.

Tip the roasted rhubarb into a blender, then add the strained sugar syrup. Blitz until smooth, then transfer into a freezer-proof container and refrigerate overnight to allow the flavour to mature.

The next day, if you have an ice-cream maker, churn the sorbet for 1 hour. If not, place it in the freezer overnight or until frozen, then break up the frozen mixture and blitz in a blender until you have a smooth sorbet. Serve or freeze again.

Avocado &
Cardamom
Ice Cream

The first time Bibi saw me eating avocado on toast, she couldn't believe what she had seen. She gave it a try, and was not impressed at all. She told me that in Zanzibar, they grew avocados as big as my head and only ate them sweet. The concept of a savoury avocado was unbelievable to her; it was always a pudding for them, often blended with ice until it was something between a smoothie and ice cream – almost like a smoothie bowl. So here is her super-simple, fuss-free avocado ice cream, with my addition of coconut flakes.

Serves 4

2 large, ripe avocados, peeled,
    stoned and sliced
170g (scant 6oz) evaporated milk
45g (scant ¼ cup) caster
    (superfine) sugar
½ tsp ground cardamom
    (optional)
75g (2½oz) coconut flakes

Combine all the ingredients except the coconut flakes in a blender and blend until smooth.

Pour into a freezer-proof container and leave to freeze overnight.

Before serving, briefly toast the coconut flakes in a frying pan over a medium heat until they turn golden.

Divide the avocado ice cream between four bowls, then sprinkle the coconut flakes on top and serve.

Tamarind Rose

This is my mum's party drink; she always has to make it for any gathering or event. As a child, I thought it was the worst thing ever – I am so thankful my taste buds grew up! Using tamarind in a sweet way very much comes from the Zanzibari side of my family. At my first-ever supper club in London, I wanted to test this on my guests, so I decided to use my mum's recipe, but with a gentle touch of rose water. Everyone loved it, and ever since then, I always make it for my events – I guess I've turned into my mum! The rose is a total extra and not something you have to add. If you plan to keep this over a couple of days, then I would suggest making it with still water.

Serves 5–6

100g (3½oz) tamarind block
80g (6½ tbsp) caster (superfine)
    sugar
50ml (scant ¼ cup) rose water
ice cubes
1 litre (4⅓ cups) sparkling water
    (or still, if you prefer)

Soak the tamarind in 140ml (scant ⅔ cup) of boiling water and leave for about 2 hours or overnight.

After soaking, your tamarind should have softened, and if you squeeze it with your hands, it will form a pulp. Strain the pulp through a sieve to remove the seeds, then transfer to a blender.

Add the sugar and rose water to the blender, along with a few ice cubes, and blitz for 30 seconds until combined, then stir in the sparkling water.

Pour into a bottle and refrigerate for at least an hour until chilled, then serve over ice. This will keep in the fridge for up to a week.

Sherbati

Rose, Chia & Almond
Milkshake

Serves 5–6

1 litre (4⅓ cups) almond milk
75g (6 tbsp) caster
    (superfine) sugar
150ml (⅔ cup) rose syrup
seeds scraped from ½ vanilla pod,
    or 1 tsp vanilla extract
ice cubes
2 tsp chia seeds or basil seeds
75g (2½oz) pistachios,
    finely chopped

When I spoke about the Zanzibar street-food market on page 166, I mentioned how Bibi and her brother Gigi used to visit Forodhani park in Stone Town with their dad and watch the police band play as they drank their *sherbati* from Uncle Habib. Well, here is their *sherbati*! It's also a drink we make during Muharram, the first month of the Islamic new year. A big batch is made, bottled up and donated to little kids in Zanzibar. It's essentially a rose-flavoured milkshake. The traditional version was made much sweeter with condensed milk and basil seeds, which bloom and become gelatinous, like chia seeds. My Auntie Rayhana, a very good family friend who was born in Uganda to a Gujarati family, also used to have this as a child. Since she started making it here in the UK, she has found that it tastes much better with almond milk. The most important tip for this is to make sure it's super cold when serving, just like a milkshake!

Combine the almond milk, sugar, rose syrup and vanilla in a blender. Add 4–5 ice cubes and blend until smooth.

Add the chia seeds and leave them to bloom for at least 5 minutes until they have become jelly-like.

Pour over ice, then sprinkle the pistachios on top of each glass.

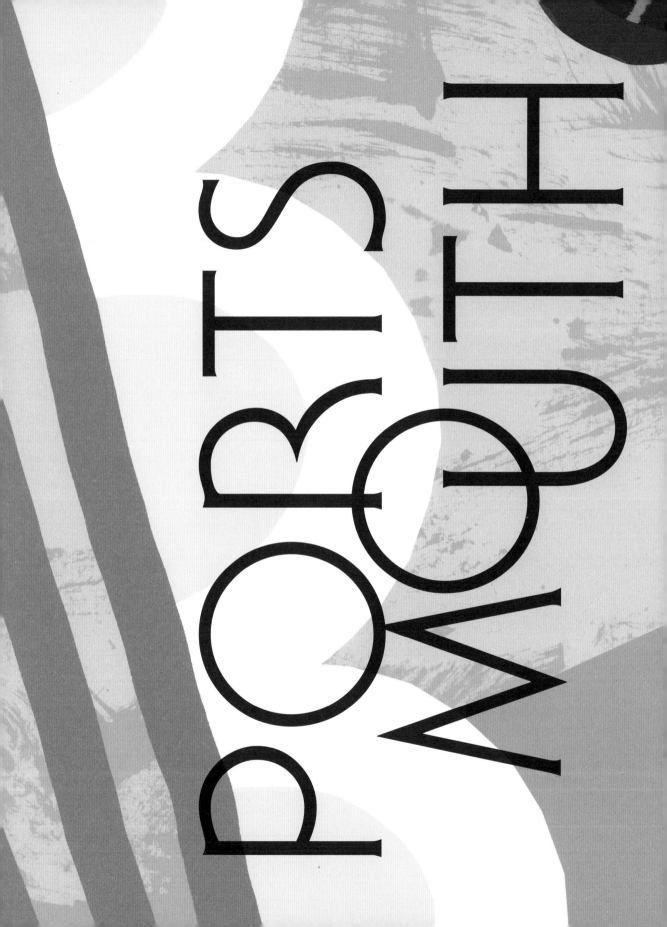

I have always had a love/hate relationship with the city of Portsmouth, but this is the place that gave me my essence. It has shaped me into the person I am today, and it's the place where much of my food career began. This was where my mother and grandmother shared their recipes with me, giving me the freedom to express my identity and the chance to play with local produce to recreate my family's food in the UK. This chapter is a glimpse into Dina – the recipes that make up the different parts of my heritage and upbringing.

Spinach &
Coconut
Shakshuka

Serves 4

6 tbsp olive oil or vegetable oil
1 onion, thinly sliced
2 garlic cloves, finely chopped
1 tsp ground turmeric
1 tsp ground cumin
3 tomatoes, finely diced
600g (1lb 5oz) spinach
400ml (14fl oz) can of coconut milk
1 green chilli (optional)
juice of 1 lime
salt, to taste
handful of fresh coriander
    (cilantro), chopped
4 eggs
pomegranate seeds,
    to garnish (optional)
black olives, to garnish (optional)

This shakshuka is based on a Zanzibari dish known as *mchicha* or *mboga*, which means "spinach" or "vegetables" in Swahili (see page 159 for my version). If you mention these names, we instantly know the dish will be made with coconut. Coconut forms the base of many Zanzibari dishes, and is often used as a substitute for water. Although *mchicha* tastes amazing, it isn't the most showstopping dish to look at, so I decided to use *mchicha* as a base for shakshuka, to help people fall in love with some of our home comforts. Serve with toast.

Heat the olive oil in a large frying pan over a medium heat. Add the onions and garlic and sweat for 3–4 minutes, then stir in the ground spices. Then add the tomatoes and fry for another 5–6 minutes. Next add the spinach, a handful at a time, and fry for 5 minutes until it has all wilted.

Pour in the coconut milk, then add the chilli and lime juice. Season with salt and leave to simmer for 20 minutes until the coconut has thickened and there is little liquid left.

Add the coriander and stir well, then leave to simmer for another 3–4 minutes.

Make 4 holes in the spinach mixture and crack an egg into each hole. Cover the pan with a lid and leave the eggs to cook through for 5 minutes, until the egg whites are cooked and you have a runny yolk (or you can leave it for longer to get a hard yolk, if you prefer!).

Sprinkle over the pomegranates and/or olives, if using, and serve.

Mama's Coconut Dhal

Serves 4–5

5 tbsp olive oil
1 tbsp black mustard seeds
1 onion, finely chopped
½ tsp garlic paste
½ tsp ginger paste
2 red chillies, finely chopped
1 tsp ground cumin
1 tsp ground coriander
1 tsp freshly ground black pepper
½ tsp ground turmeric
1 tomato, diced
200g (7oz) red lentils
400ml (14fl oz) can of coconut milk
1 tsp salt
juice of 1 lemon
crispy fried onions,
   to serve (optional)

Once in a while, my mum wakes up on the weekend and decides we are having dhal for breakfast. In Oman, it's a very common breakfast item at local restaurants, served with steaming hot flaky paratha. Whenever my cousin Khadija and I head off on a road trip in Oman, we always grab a pot of dhal with paratha and sit in the car to eat it, trying our hardest not to stain our clothes with turmeric. We then begin our journey with very full stomachs and question why we ate so much, but dhal is so delicious and comforting that even in 40°C (104°F) heat, we just can't resist! Of course, with my mother's Zanzibari influence, we have it with coconut. A creamy, easy dish that you can have at any time of the day.

Heat the oil in a medium-large saucepan over a medium-high heat. Add the mustard seeds and fry for 2–3 minutes until they start to pop, then add the onion, garlic and ginger pastes, chillies and ground spices, and sauté for about 8–10 minutes until the onions begin to turn light brown.

Stir in the tomato and sauté for another 5 minutes until softened, then add the lentils, coconut milk and 1 litre (4⅓ cups) of water. Add the salt, then reduce the heat to medium and simmer for 30 minutes until the mixture has thickened and the lentils are cooked.

Stir in the lemon juice and simmer for a further 5 minutes, then serve topped with the crispy onions.

Bibi's Famous Biriyani

Serves 6

1–2 litres (4⅓–8½ cups) vegetable oil, for deep-frying

1.5kg (3lb 3oz) onions, thinly sliced

5 tablespoons baharat spice blend (see page 120) or garam masala

250g (9oz) tomato purée

750g (1lb 10oz) mutton, cut into 5–7.5cm (2–3in) chunks, ideally on the bone

50g (1¾oz) garlic paste

50g (1¾oz) ginger paste

500g (2 cups) plain yogurt

1 tbsp salt

2 large potatoes, each chopped into 4–6 chunks

juice of 4 lemons

450g (2¼ cups) basmati rice

3 pinches of saffron strands

1 tbsp granulated sugar

Bibi and my grandfather, Babu, moved to the UK in April 1965. Bibi had fled Zanzibar by boat in the night with her five children one year before, going to Mombasa, Kenya. She had told her friends and family they were going on holiday, as she couldn't risk revealing that they were running away before things got worse on the island. My mum was around four years old when they left, and to this day she has a vivid memory of the security guard at the port confiscating her big brother Nasser's money box. Due to the ongoing conflict, you were not allowed to leave with anything of value, just your clothes.

Meanwhile, my grandfather had been sent to New York by the Zanzibari government on a scholarship to study food canning. The scholarship couldn't have come at a better point; Babu was part of the Arab political party against whom the Afro-Shirazi party was fighting. Had Babu stayed, he probably wouldn't have lived to see his children grow up.

It was a scary journey for Bibi, having to stay helpless in Mombasa until they could get their papers for the UK, but once they made it, their community was there, waiting to help them rebuild their lives. Even Bibi's best friends from the royal family had to begin afresh. Together, Bibi tells me, all the men and women went out to find work, though they didn't speak much English. Most of them got their first jobs at a bottle factory called Metal Box, and this is where their new life began: a group of Zanzibaris packing bottles to build a future.

Although there are not many Omani-Zanzibaris left in Portsmouth today, as people have passed away or moved back to Oman, when I was growing up there in the 1990s, the community was thriving. Wherever I turned, there was someone I could call an auntie, uncle or cousin – even if they weren't blood relatives, our bond came from a shared sense of belonging. Evenings and weekends were always spent visiting Bibi and Babu's friends; within our new homes, their island was recreated.

Every year without fail, the whole community would come together to celebrate Eid. Everyone made an effort. The women would decide among themselves who would cook what, while the men were on hand to bring all the huge stainless-steel saucepans full of home-cooked delights down to our local multicultural centre.

Bibi made the best biriyani, and everyone knew it. In the lead-up to Eid, she could easily spend a whole week frying onions – mainly because as soon as she fried them, everyone who came to the house would snack on them! This dish has always been her showstopper; the minute there is a celebration, it's the only thing she wants to cook. Those get-togethers just amplified her biriyani ego – but then again, with a mouthful of Bibi's biriyani and a community so tight, we all had something worth boasting about.

Recipe continues overleaf

Begin by frying the onions. Pour the oil into a large saucepan to a depth of 10–15cm (4–6in). Add half the onions at room temperature; they need to be fully covered in the oil. Place over a high heat and fry for 15 minutes until golden brown. Be sure to keep turning and moving the onions in the pan so they don't burn. Once the onions are cooked, transfer to a tray, but do not line it with kitchen paper (paper towels), as we don't want them to drain. Add the second batch of onions to the oil and fry for 6–8 minutes; this batch will cook faster as the oil is already hot.

While the onions are frying, begin cooking the meat. In a large, deep, ovenproof pan, combine 3 tablespoons of the baharat with the tomato purée, meat, garlic and ginger pastes and yogurt. Add the salt and place over a high heat. Once it starts to bubble, reduce the heat to low. Cover with a tightly fitting lid and leave to simmer for 30 minutes.

After 30 minutes, add the potatoes, along with 100ml (scant ½ cup) of water if the pan is looking a little dry, then cover and cook for a further 30 minutes. Then add the lemon juice and a third of the fried onions. Stir well and leave to cook for another 20 minutes.

Preheat the oven to 200° C (180° C/400° F/Gas 6).

While the sauce is cooking, parboil the rice. Fill a saucepan with enough water to cover the rice. Season with salt and bring to the boil, then add the rice. Leave it to cook for 10–15 minutes until the rice is soft, but not completely cooked (keep the lid off). Make sure the water isn't all absorbed. Drain the rice and set aside.

When the meat is cooked and starting to become tender, taste the sauce and add some more salt if needed. Sprinkle the remaining 2 tablespoons of baharat over the top of the sauce, followed by another third of the onions, then add the parboiled rice on top.

Grind the saffron and sugar using a pestle and mortar to make a powder. Add 50ml (scant ¼ cup) of boiling water and stir well to make an infusion.

Use a spoon to make holes in the rice layer, then pour the saffron infusion over the top, making sure some goes into the holes. Next, pour 2 ladlefuls of the onion oil from the pan over the rice, before topping with the rest of the onions.

Cover the top of the pan with a piece of foil to lock in the steam, then top with the lid. Transfer to the oven for 1 hour.

When you're ready to serve, spoon the rice on to the plates first, then dig deeper into the pan to get the meat/masala part. Serve with your chosen accompaniments.

Cooking notes:

You can use lamb, chicken, or vegetables (like parsnips, carrots or cauliflower) if you prefer; the cooking time will be shorter. Lamb and mutton on the bone will yield the best flavour for the stock.

Serve this with plain yogurt. We like to mix the yogurt with cucumber, coriander (cilantro), onions, tomatoes, raisins and salt. You can use coconut yogurt for a dairy-free alternative if you like, but try to get one that is not strong in flavour. This also pairs well with a citrussy, leafy salad.

Left Bibi and Babu in Southsea; ***above*** Bibi barbecuing; ***below*** at a family gathering in Oman.

IRAN & OMAN

My grandmother loves to reminisce about Iran. She remembers the time of the Shah, when Iran was in its mystique era. Iran radiated beauty, glitz and glamour; it was simply the place to be. Bibi migrated to Iran from Portsmouth in 1974, when my grandfather was offered a job there. Although Bibi had five children back in the UK, that did not stop her from going off to live her best life in Tehran. She packed her bags, called her mother to come and look after her brood, and went off for two years with her husband to revel in her fantasy of a culture with which she identified, but had never truly experienced; a lot like myself and Oman. Both my maternal grandparents had fathers with Iranian heritage, so Bibi's obsession with Iran stemmed from a desire to better understand herself.

Iran features heavily in the history of the north of Oman, since Iran occupied or annexed parts of Muscat and the Al Batinah region in around 500 BCE, returning in the fifth and sixth centuries CE when the Sasanian Empire (the last pre-Islamic Persian empire) settled there, and again in the 18th century, finally leaving in 1744. Iran returned to Oman an ally in 1972, when the emperor sent 15,000 soldiers to support the Sultan with the Dhofar conflict, when separatists from the southern region of Dhofar fought against the government. This conflict arose during a time of great strife and scarcity, driven by a Pan-Arabic movement influenced by Marxist ideology that was sweeping the region.

There was also a port city in Iran known as Bandar Abbas that came under the control of the Sultanate of Oman & Zanzibar between 1794 and 1868, along with a 100-mile stretch of the coast and a couple of islands. This is where most of the Iranian *qabeyel* (see page 22) now in Oman originally came from.

Left, below Bibi and Babu;
above Bibi and Babu with friends in
Portsmouth in the early 1970s.

I would describe the historical relationship between Oman and Iran as being much like the one between my grandparents: some fighting and need for power, a tendency towards overruling one another, yet ultimately long-lasting and very close – close enough to share cultural traditions while also creating new *qabeyel* that represent both of them. To better understand how close Oman and Iran literally are, if you stand in Musandam, the most northern point of Oman, on a clear, blue day, you may be able to see Iran and its islands in the distance; you might even manage to connect to their phone service!

Oman and Iran are forever connected by the *bahari* (ocean). They share the Strait of Hormuz, which is now one of the most significant oil chokepoints in the world; about 21 million barrels of oil pass through it every day – roughly a third of the world's daily supply. But long before oil took on the significance it has today, it was this strait that brought us together. Both countries moved back and forth fluidly, conquering and exchanging influences through architecture, produce, language and cuisine.

Which brings me to *fesenjoon*. Originating from Gilan in the north of Iran, *fesenjoon* is a celebratory dish traditionally made with pomegranate molasses, ground walnuts and wild duck; the marriage of flavours created by so few ingredients is extraordinary. It's so wonderful, in fact, that when my maternal grandfather's cousins moved from Iran to Zanzibar in the 1940s, they made sure they found a way to replicate the dish for their family. However, Zanzibar didn't grow walnuts, so they had to work with what they had. One thing that did grow in abundance was cashews – and, just like that, a couple of women filled with curiosity and cravings took an Iranian classic and made it Iranian-Zanzibari. And that's the beauty of food, isn't it? How far dishes travel, and how widely they are adapted as people migrate across borders and seas.

The first time my grandmother introduced me to this dish, she told me that when they moved to England in 1965, she couldn't find any of their Zanzibari staple ingredients – even cashew nuts seemed to be non-existent, and if you were lucky enough to find some, the price was more than unpleasant, especially when feeding a household of seven. So, once again, she adapted, worked with what she had, and used peanut butter. I greatly admire my grandmother's resilience, and her intuition for cooking what she knew and loved. I guess that is partly where I got my passion for playing with food: from a woman who had no choice but to experiment in order to stay grounded to her roots. So, while this is a truly delicious stew, what I really love about this recipe is how it symbolises deep-rooted history, and the challenges faced by the great women who have handed it down to me. I've shared my version on page 209.

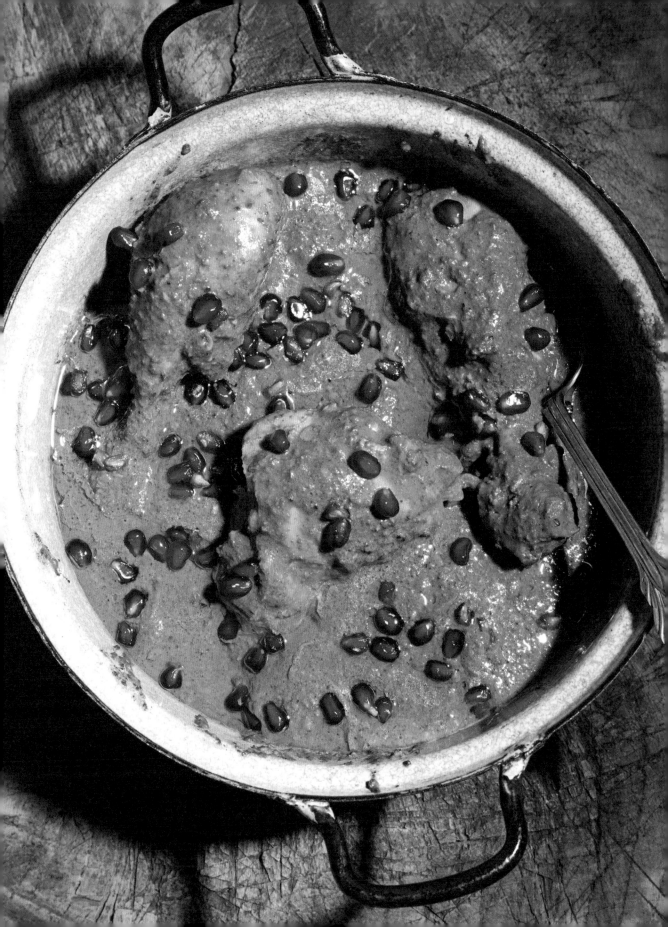

Fesenjoon

Cashew & Pomegranate
Chicken Stew

Serves 4

250g (9oz) unsalted cashew nuts
6 tbsp neutral oil, such as light
    vegetable oil
1 onion, thinly sliced
145g (5¼oz) pomegranate
    molasses
150ml (⅔ cup) pomegranate juice
1 whole chicken, about 1.5kg
    (3lb 3oz), cut into 8 pieces,
    skin removed (or you can
    use precut skinless pieces,
    ideally on the bone)
1 tsp ground turmeric
2 tbsp garlic paste
2 tsp freshly ground black pepper
1–2 tsp salt
fresh pomegranate seeds,
    to garnish

I've kept this recipe as true to the original as possible. Although the dish is traditionally made with duck, my family has always used chicken. I'm not sure they ever even *saw* a duck in Zanzibar... Chicken on the bone is essential here, as the stock from the bones really elevates the flavours; using a premade stock would simply overpower it. I always enjoy this most the next day, when the flavours have had a chance to deepen, but as long as you have given yourself enough time to start this before dinner, it will still be just perfect. I always serve this with *tahdig* (crispy bottom rice, see page 210 for my version) or saffron rice.

Preheat the oven to 180°C (160°C fan/350°F/Gas 4).

Spread out the cashew nuts on a baking tray and roast in the oven for 15 minutes until they have deepened in colour. Check on them after 10 minutes, and give them a shake about so they don't burn. Once roasted, transfer to a food processor and blitz to form a fine crumb, then set aside.

Heat the oil in a large saucepan over a medium–high heat. Add the onion and sauté for 10 minutes until translucent, then stir in the ground cashews and fry for 2 minutes more.

Pour in 2 litres (8½ cups) of water, and whisk thoroughly to make sure the cashew nuts don't clump together. Cover with the lid and leave to simmer over a medium heat for 1 hour.

After this time, check on the contents of the pan. The water will have started to change colour and become slightly opaque. You want to keep stewing the cashew water until it deepens in colour, so continue to simmer for another 1 hour.

Now add another 1 litre (4⅓ cups) water, as well as the pomegranate molasses and juice. Stir well to combine, then leave to simmer for another hour.

Finally, add the chicken, turmeric, garlic paste, black pepper and salt. Stir, then leave to cook for another 40 minutes until the chicken is cooked through and is tender.

When serving, scatter over fresh pomegranate seeds to garnish.

Plantain &
Barberry
Tahdig Rice

Serves 4–5

2 pinches of saffron strands
3 tsp caster (superfine) sugar
80g (2¾oz) ghee, melted
50g (1¾oz) barberries or
    cranberries, finely chopped
    if using cranberries
1 large ripe plantain, about
    250–300g (9–10½oz), peeled
    and sliced into 2.5cm (1in) slices
    (whatever shape you like)
300g (1½ cups) basmati
    rice, rinsed
1–2 tsp salt
20g (¾oz) parsley, finely chopped

Tahdig (which means "bottom of the pot" in Farsi) is a traditional Iranian recipe where rice is slow-cooked until it has a crispy bottom. We make it in Oman and Zanzibar – we call the crispy part the *koqwa* in Swahili, which translates as "fruit stone", or *hakuuka* or *haraqah* in Omani Arabic, which means "to scratch the bottom of the pan".

    This version of *tahdig* rice has no real origin, but is a mishmash of my own making that plays on the beauty of being from everywhere and nowhere. The plantain element is very much my addition. In Zanzibar and other parts of East Africa, it is always a "thing" to eat rice dishes with a banana. You can serve this with roasted meat or even a curry if you like. It's just another way to have fun with your rice.

Using a pestle and mortar, pound the saffron strands with 1 teaspoon of the sugar until they form a powder, then pour over 2 tablespoons of hot water and set aside.

Melt 10g (¼oz) of the ghee in a frying pan over a medium heat. Add the barberries or cranberries and sauté for 2–3 minutes, then pour in 50ml (scant ¼ cup) of water, along with the remaining sugar. Simmer for 5 minutes to let the water evaporate, then remove from the pan and set aside in a bowl.

Return the pan to a medium heat and add another 40g (1⅓oz) of the ghee. Once it has melted, arrange the plantain slices over the base of the pan. Cook for 2–3 minutes until they turn golden, then flip them over and remove from the heat. They will cook on the other side later.

Place the rice in a large saucepan and pour in enough water to cover the rice by about 5cm (2in). Add the salt, then bring to the boil over a high heat. Leave to bubble for around 5 minutes to parboil, then drain, making sure to reserve some of the water.

Mix the rice with the barberries or cranberries and parsley, then tip it into the frying pan on top of the plantain. Make sure it is pressed in well, with no gaps. Using the back of a spoon, make about 6–8 holes in the rice.

Add about 2 tablespoons of the reserved rice water to the saffron mixture, then pour this over the rice, making sure it goes into the holes. Finally, take the remaining 30g (1oz) of the ghee and spread it over the top and into the holes.

Securely wrap a clean tea towel around the lid of the frying pan, then place it on top of the pan to lock in the steam, making sure it's tight. Place over a low heat and leave to cook for about an hour; depending on your hob, you might need to use a slightly higher heat.

Once ready, take a plate and carefully flip the rice on to it to serve. You should be rewarded with a crispy and caramelised *tahdig* base.

Mum's Leftover Christmas Shuwarmas

Makes 6 wraps

4–5 leftover roast potatoes,
   halved
4 tbsp olive oil, plus extra for
   drizzling
2 tbsp ground cumin
1 tsp freshly ground black pepper
1 red onion, thinly sliced
430g (15oz) turkey/goose leftovers,
   shredded (or any cooked meat)
20g (¾oz) coriander (cilantro),
   chopped
6 baby pitta or small tortilla
   breads
pomegranate seeds, to garnish

For the carrots
2 tbsp granulated sugar
50ml (scant ¼ cup) red
   wine vinegar
1 tsp salt, plus extra for sprinkling
145g (5¼oz) leftover roasted
   carrots, or other leftover
   roasted veg

For the mint-sauce tahini
3 tbsp tahini
1½ tbsp mint sauce/jelly
3 tbsp plain yogurt
pinch of salt
lemon juice, to taste

For the cranberry salsa
2 tomatoes, roughly chopped
3 tbsp cranberry jelly
1 fresh red or green chilli,
   finely chopped
pinch of salt

One year, my cousins came to visit us from Oman. They happened to be with us over Christmas, and while they were excited to experience some of the festivities they had seen on TV, they were not so impressed with Christmas lunch. They were used to home-cooked Omani food, so the concept of roasted veg, lashings of gravy and no rice at the table was alien to them. They spent the rest of the day snacking on nibbles and sweets, and the next morning I remember waking up to the aroma of frying onions and meat. It turned out to be my mother refusing to accept that my cousins didn't like her roast; she had decided to use up her leftovers and make something they were more familiar with. Thus, her Leftover Christmas Shuwarmas with mint-sauce tahini and cranberry chilli salsa were born. Since then, every Boxing Day (or Monday after a Sunday roast) has featured these, and they are blooming epic.

Preheat the oven to 210°C (190°C fan/410°F/Gas 6½).

Start with the carrots. Combine the sugar, vinegar and 1 teaspoon of salt in a small saucepan over a high heat. Once it reaches boiling point, leave it to simmer for 5 minutes until the sugar dissolves, then add the carrots and mix well. Leave on the heat for a further minute, then set aside to cool completely. This will make a nice roast carrot pickle.

Chop your leftover roast potatoes into small cubes or French fry shapes, then place on a baking tray and drizzle with olive oil. Roast for 15 minutes until crunchy, then set aside to cool.

In a small bowl, combine all the ingredients for the mint-sauce tahini. Mix well and set aside.

Combine all the cranberry salsa ingredients in a blender. Blend until smooth, then set aside.

Heat the 4 tablespoons of oil in a frying pan over a medium heat. Add the ground cumin and black pepper. Once sizzling, sauté for 2 minutes, then add the onion and sweat for a further 5 minutes.

Add the shredded meat and fry off for another 6–8 minutes (if using raw meat, cook for longer until cooked through), then add three-quarters of the chopped coriander. Stir well to combine, then take off the heat.

With all your shuwarma elements ready, it is time to assemble. I like to heat my bread in a dry frying pan for a few seconds, then coat the inside with a layer of mint-sauce tahini, followed by the carrots, meat mixture, potatoes and lastly the cranberry salsa. Scatter over a few extra coriander leaves and, if you have them (which I always do), some pomegranate seeds. Then wrap it all up and enjoy.

Above, left my mum, Kamila, at home in Portsmouth in the 1980s; **above, right** Mum when she was living in Oman in the 1980s; **left** Mum visiting Mirbat, in the south of Oman.

Pakora
Scotch Egg

Makes 4

4 fresh eggs
400g (14oz) minced (ground)
    meat (I use beef or lamb)
1 red onion
1–2 fresh red chillies (optional)
1 tbsp baharat spice blend (see
    page 120)
35g (1¼oz) coriander (cilantro)
2 tsp salt
vegetable oil, for deep-frying

For the pakora batter
135g (1 cup) gram flour
1 tsp ground turmeric
1 tsp salt
1 tsp baking powder
1 onion, thinly sliced

Tip:

Please use super-fresh, good quality
free-range eggs – it makes such a
difference to the flavour.

There is much debate around the Scotch egg – trying to establish its origins is more confusing than learning if the chicken or the egg came first! British history tells us that the snack originated in Yorkshire in the 1800s; Indians will tell you that they, in fact, were making it long before, and call it *narjis kofta* (*narjis* in Arabic is the name of the narcissus flower, referencing the yellow middle and white exterior). Tunisians also have their own version, called *tajine sebnekh*, which translates as "spinach tagine", as they cover the egg in a creamed spinach. Then you have us, the Zanzibaris, who – Bibi says – have always made them, calling them *kababu za mayai*, which literally translates as "kebab of eggs". These are made using beef mince and about six different spices, and are usually covered in potato before deep-frying.

Bibi tells me that when they first moved to Portsmouth, she came across a bakery selling Scotch eggs, and was amazed to find something that looked familiar. For months, she would buy loads of them, always complaining about how under-seasoned they were, but eating them for the "Zanzibar-esque" comfort – only to one day discover to her horror that they were made with pork and not beef!

She taught me how they used to make them on the island, using desiccated coconut instead of breadcrumbs when they didn't have bread to waste. While Bibi's way is fabulous, I've kept her mince recipe the same and changed the exterior to something more exciting. My mum and I love to experiment in the kitchen, and one of our favourite things to do is to see what random ingredient we can add to a pakora. It just so happens that on one of these occasions, we dipped a whole Scotch egg in the pakora batter. It was very messy, but so worth it!

Begin by boiling your eggs. If you have your own preferred method, please go ahead and use that. I usually bring my water to the boil in a saucepan, then add my eggs and boil for exactly 5 minutes, then transfer to cold water to stop cooking. This will give you perfectly runny yolks. Set aside.

To prepare the pakora batter, combine the dry ingredients in a large bowl, followed by 120ml (½ cup) of water. As you mix it, the mixture should come together as a thick mess/paste. Add another 4 tablespoons of water and whisk until there are no lumps; aim for the consistency of pancake batter. Now stir through the onion and set aside.

Recipe continues overleaf

In a food processor, combine the mince, red onion, chillies (if using), baharat and coriander. Season with the salt and blitz until everything is finely chopped and you have a smooth texture. If you don't have a food processor, you'll need to chop the chillies, onion and coriander as finely as possible, then use your hands to mix everything together.

Now everything is prepped, pour oil into a deep saucepan to a depth of 15cm (6in) and place over a high heat.

While the oil is heating up, carefully peel your boiled eggs, then take a handful of mince and flatten it out in the palm of your hand, making it as thin as you can without it breaking apart. Place one of the peeled eggs in the middle and wrap the mince around it, being careful not to squeeze the egg too much. Make sure the egg is completely covered. If the mix is loose around the egg, then you probably have too much, so just pinch off some of the mince.

Check that your saucepan of oil is hot. You can check that the oil is ready by dropping in a small dollop of the batter; if it cooks instantly, the oil is ready.

Now dip the wrapped eggs into the pakora batter, ready to fry. With this, you want to get an even layer of batter and onion around the egg. Instead of trying to roll it around in the batter, sit the egg in the batter, then pick up some onion slices and place them on top. As you lift each egg out of the batter, catch some of the onion slices underneath it too, and quickly transfer it to the hot oil. Once the eggs touch the hot oil, the onion batter will instantly stick and cook, and you should come out with an even coating of pakora batter.

Fry the eggs for 2–4 minutes until golden. This will be long enough to cook the mince, as it should be just a thin layer. Repeat with the remaining eggs, meat and batter, then enjoy.

Pomegranate & Honey Beef Short Ribs

Serves 3–4

3 tbsp olive oil
1 onion, thinly sliced
3 garlic cloves, finely chopped
1kg (2¼lb) beef short ribs
 (not too much fat)
100g (3½oz) pomegranate
 molasses
85g (3oz) runny honey
1 tbsp baharat spice blend (see
 page 120)
3 thyme sprigs
salt

Any chance I get to add pomegranates to something, I will do it. This recipe was one of my first introductions to eating ribs; I had never been a fan, but this converted me. My mum and I enjoy these ribs as our favourite comfort food; we stick them in the slow cooker and just forget about them as they become tender and irresistible. Sometimes, we even leave them stewing overnight and wake up to have them with avocado on toast for breakfast! These go with anything. We'll eat them with white rice or French fries, or sometimes with a roast dinner. They're totally versatile and always fun!

Preheat the oven to 180°C (160°C fan/350°F/Gas 4).

Heat the oil in a large ovenproof pan over a medium heat. Add the onion and sauté for 10 minutes, then add the garlic and ribs. Brown the ribs for about 15 minutes on each side.

Once browned, add the molasses, honey, baharat, thyme and 125ml (generous ½ cup) of water. Season with salt to taste. Stir together, then place a large piece of foil on top of the pan, followed by a lid, so that it is tightly sealed. Transfer to the oven for 2½ hours.

Once cooked, the meat should be tender and falling off the bone. There may be a layer of fat on top of the sauce; you can spoon that off. Using a ladle, remove about three-quarters of the liquid and reduce in a saucepan over a low heat for 15 minutes until it thickens and becomes like a sticky glaze.

Pour the glaze over the ribs and serve.

Cooking notes:

Try to avoid beef ribs with too much fat. You want some, but not loads.

Use an ovenproof pan, as these start on the hob and end up in the oven. I prefer to make them in a slow cooker or instant pot to save energy and time, so if you have one, give that a try.

Brown Butter
& Saffron
Scallops

Serves 4

good pinch of saffron
1 tsp granulated sugar
70g (scant 5 tbsp) salted butter,
    chopped into 1cm (¾in) cubes
good pinch of sea salt
½ tsp freshly ground black pepper
16 scallops
large handful of dill
squeeze of lemon juice

During 2020, while stuck back home in Portsmouth for lockdown, I developed a love for cycling down the beach – and always ended up at the fishmongers. I had always loved eating scallops, but hadn't ever really cooked them at home; they just seemed like the type of seafood a restaurant needed to make for me. So that year, I started bringing back some scallops every week until I could get them just right. It turns out they are actually super easy to make and are a very quick and simple crowd-pleaser.

Using a pestle and mortar, pound the saffron strands and sugar until they form a powder. Add 2 tablespoons of boiling water and leave this mixture to sit while you prepare the rest.

Melt 4 cubes of the butter with the salt and pepper in a small frying pan over a medium–high heat.

Add your scallops to the pan. Increase the heat to high and sear the scallops for about 2 minutes without turning, until they start to change colour.

Add the rest of the butter, along with the saffron mixture, and let the butter melt down with the heat still on high. Once the butter has melted down, reduce the heat slightly and turn the scallops over to cook on the other side for 4–6 minutes. During this time, the butter will brown. Foam will appear and the milk fats will fall to the bottom and toast. Use a spoon to keep moving the butter around, pouring it on top of the scallops.

When everything is ready, remove the pan from the heat. Add the dill, and squeeze in the lemon, then briefly stir and serve right away.

Cooking notes:

Make sure to cut the butter into small cubes so it browns evenly in the pan.

I use a small frying pan so I can create a pool of butter for the scallops.

Sticky Tamarind Fried Chicken Wings

These are the type of wings that make you want to take off your clothes, sit at a table, tie a bib around you and get messy. No cutlery is needed, just hands. This recipe came about one Ramadan, when we had loads of extra tamarind sauce for all our little bites. I love the dip so much that I will douse whatever I can find in it! That day, I had craved KFC, so I decided to pour some of this tamarind sauce over some hot wings. In that moment, I had never been so proud of myself.

Serves 4

1kg (2¼lb) chicken wings, halved
1 tsp ground cumin
½ tsp cayenne pepper
2 tsp garlic paste
1 tsp ginger paste
1–2 tsp salt
vegetable oil, for deep-frying

For the tamarind sauce
60g (2oz) tamarind block
30g (1oz) date molasses
30g (1oz) runny honey
1 tsp salt
1 fresh chilli
2 tomatoes, about 150g (5½oz),
    roughly chopped
10g (¼oz) coriander (cilantro)
10g (¼oz) mint leaves

For the batter
200g (generous 1½ cups)
    plain flour
300ml (1¼ cups) tonic or
    sparkling water
1 large egg, beaten
½ tsp chilli powder
1 tsp onion powder
1 tsp salt

Before you begin, soak the tamarind in 300ml (1¼ cups) of water in a bowl for at least 1 hour or overnight.

When you're ready to start cooking, place the chicken wings in a large bowl and add the cumin, cayenne pepper, garlic and ginger pastes and salt. Mix well to coat and leave to marinate while you prepare the sauce.

Your tamarind should have softened and absorbed the water; if you squeeze it with your hands, it will form a pulp. Strain the pulp through a sieve to remove the seeds, taking care not to lose too much of the tamarind. Once strained, transfer to a saucepan.

Add the rest of the tamarind sauce ingredients to the pan, then place over a medium heat and bring to a light simmer for 10 minutes. The sauce should reduce slightly and become thicker. Set aside and leave to cool completely.

Combine all your batter ingredients in a large bowl and whisk together until smooth.

Pour oil into a large saucepan to a depth of 10–12cm (4–5in) and place over a high heat. While the oil is heating up, drop the marinated chicken wings into the batter and turn to coat well.

To check if the oil is hot enough for frying, drop in a small dollop of batter. If it rises straight away and starts to sizzle, the oil is ready. Once the oil is hot enough, drop in the battered chicken pieces, working in batches so as not to overcrowd the pan. Fry for around 3 minutes on each side until golden, then set aside on a plate lined with kitchen paper (paper towels) to drain the excess oil while you fry the rest.

Once all the wings have been fried, dip them in the batter once more and fry again for extra crunch, working in batches as before.

After all the wings have been double-fried, arrange them in a serving bowl and pour over the tamarind sauce. Toss well to coat, and serve immediately. If you prefer, you can serve the sauce on the side, instead.

Pomegranate & Mango Chicken Wings

~~~~~~

Serves 4

1kg (2¼lb) chicken wings (skin on)
80g (2¾oz) pomegranate
　molasses
2 fresh mangoes, about 480g
　(1lb 10oz) in total, flesh blended
　into a pulp
2 tbsp baharat spice blend (see
　page 120)
　or garam masala
juice of 1 lemon
4 tbsp olive oil
1–2 tsp salt
handful of coriander
　(cilantro), chopped
pomegranate seeds,
　to garnish (optional)

This is another way of me exercising my love for pomegranates. Simple, easy chicken wings, packed with a sweet, sour flavour.

Place the chicken wings in a large bowl and add all the other ingredients except the coriander and pomegranate seeds.

Using either your hands or a spoon, mix very well. Once the mixture has come together and the wings are coated evenly, cover the bowl with cling film (plastic wrap) and refrigerate for at least 1 hour or overnight. You can cook these right away, but I always enjoy them more when they have had time to marinate.

When you're ready to cook, preheat the oven to 220°C (200°C fan/ 425°F/Gas 7). Arrange the chicken wings on a non-stick baking tray and pour over any marinade left in the bowl. Cover with foil, then transfer to the oven and cook for 30 minutes.

After 30 minutes, remove the foil and return to the oven for another 15 minutes. The chicken wings should be starting to brown, and the skin will start to crisp up. Remove from the oven and turn the wings over, then return to the oven and roast for a further 15–20 minutes.

Once the wings are cooked through to your liking, remove from the oven and leave them to rest for about 5 minutes before serving. To serve, arrange on a platter and scatter over the coriander and pomegranate seeds.

Tip:

If I have any wings leftover, I shred the meat and serve it up in a salad the next day!

Za'atar Smashed Potato & Brie Salad with Raspberry Vinaigrette

I'm not a fan of lettuce in salads. I'd much rather have fruit in there, and have fun experimenting with different ingredients – it turns a salad into an exciting meal instead of just an extra side dish. This dressing came about during the summer of lockdown, after I had successfully grown lots of herbs and raspberries at my mum's house in Portsmouth. I was walking down to Bibi's, feeling very chuffed at being able to give her some of my homegrown produce, but when I opened my bag, I was greeted by a mess of splattered raspberries mixed up with my fresh parsley leaves. I was so mad with myself, but I refused to let all that time spent watering plants everyday go to waste, so I literally ate the mashed parsley and raspberries out of my bag – and, unexpectedly, enjoyed it! I loved it so much I turned it into this recipe, because herbs and fruits are always a great idea.

Serves 3–4

100g (3½oz) spinach
40g (1⅓oz) watercress
25g (1oz) parsley, finely chopped
100g (3½oz) Brie
50g (1¾oz) walnuts or macadamia
   nuts, crushed
seeds of ½ pomegranate

For the potatoes
400g (14 oz) baby potatoes
2 tbsp za'atar blend
3 tbsp olive oil or melted ghee
salt, to taste

For the dressing
200g (7oz) raspberries
3 tbsp extra virgin olive oil
3 tbsp red wine vinegar
squeeze of lemon juice
½ red chilli (optional)
2 tsp runny honey
salt, to taste

Preheat your oven to 220° C (200° C fan/425° F/Gas 7).

Boil your potatoes in a large saucepan of salted water over a high heat for 20–25 minutes until they are soft enough to put a fork through, but not so soft you can mash them. Drain, then transfer to a roasting tray.

Using a masher or a glass, squash the potatoes so they split and become flat. Sprinkle over 1 tablespoon of the za'atar and toss to coat them all, then drizzle over the oil or ghee and toss again, making sure they are all well coated.

Roast for around 30 minutes, checking on them after 20 minutes. You may need longer, depending on your oven. We are looking for these to have a golden and crunchy exterior. Once the potatoes are ready, transfer them to a plate and sprinkle over the remaining za'atar, then toss.

To make the dressing, you can either add all the ingredients to a blender and blitz until entirely smooth or, if you prefer a bit more texture, as I do, smash all the ingredients together using a pestle and mortar until you have a juicy dressing that still has some texture from the raspberries.

To assemble the salad, arrange your leafy greens and parsley on a serving dish, followed by the potatoes and cheese. Drizzle over the dressing, then sprinkle on the nuts and pomegranate seeds before serving.

Zhoug Mung Bean Salad

~~~~~~

Serves 5–6

100g (3½oz) mung beans
pinch of salt
seeds of 1 pomegranate
5 strawberries, finely chopped
7 pink radishes, quartered
¼ cucumber, cubed

For the dressing
4 tbsp extra virgin olive oil
juice of 1 lemon
4 whole cloves
1 tsp ground cumin
1 tsp ground cardamom
1 tsp dried chilli flakes
40g (1⅓oz) coriander (cilantro)
40g (1⅓oz) parsley
10g (½oz) mint
10g (½oz) basil leaves

I feel that mung beans are a very underrated bean. We love them so much in our family, and within Oman and Zanzibar, they are widely used. While we don't usually use them in salads, I think they make a great base to one. Here, I've paired them with a homemade Yemeni herby chilli sauce more commonly known as *zhoug* but also as *bisbas*, which I love to have alongside a Yemeni rice dish known as *mandhi* when I'm in Oman. The combination of texture, herbs, fruit and tang is everything I love in a meal, so this salad is a firm favourite! You can adjust the fruit and vegetables to suit your tastes.

Soak the mung beans overnight in a bowl of boiling water. The next day, drain, then add to a saucepan, along with a pinch of salt. Pour over enough water to cover them, then place over a medium–high heat. Bring to the boil and boil for 45 minutes–1 hour until they are soft, but not so soft that they mash. You may need to top up with more water as they cook.

Meanwhile, in a food processor or blender, combine all the dressing ingredients. Season to taste with salt, then blend until smooth.

Once the mung beans are ready, drain them well, then tip into a large serving bowl. Throw in the fruit and veg, then pour over the dressing and mix through.

Fennel, Apple & Grape Salad

~~~~~~

Serves 4

150g (5½oz) giant couscous
1 fennel bulb, finely sliced
2 green apples, finely sliced
200g (7oz) red grapes, halved
½ orange, segmented
seeds of ½ pomegranate

For the dressing
½ tsp ground cumin
2 tbsp olive oil
1 ½ tbsp pomegranate molasses
juice of ½ orange
juice of ½ lemon
salt, to taste

When I was growing up, my mum and Bibi were notorious for chucking anything they found lying in the fruit bowl into our salads. Green apples have always been our way of mimicking the sourness we get from the unripe tart mangoes that grow in Zanzibar and Oman, while grapes were Bibi's alternative to using raisins. These two fruits seemed to always creep into every meal, so I decided they needed their own recipe. This salad is a simple and refreshing ode to our fruit bowl.

Half-fill a medium-sized saucepan with salted water and place over a high heat. Once it begins to boil, add the couscous and leave to cook for 8–10 minutes, then drain and set aside to cool.

Combine the fennel, apples, grapes, orange segments and pomegranate seeds in a salad bowl. Once the couscous has cooled, add this to the bowl and toss to combine.

Add all the dressing ingredients to a jar and shake well to combine.

Pour the dressing over the salad and toss through, then serve.

Za'atar & Garlic Focaccia

Serves 8

4 tsp fine sea salt

600ml (2½ cups) warm coconut milk

7g (scant ¼oz) fast-action dried yeast (1 packet)

650g (5¼ cups) plain (all-purpose) flour

1 tsp soft light brown sugar

1 egg

125ml (generous ½ cup) olive oil, plus extra for greasing the pan, and 2 tbsp for drizzling

1 tsp sea salt flakes

1 heaped tbsp za'atar blend

1 heaped tbsp dried za'atar leaves or dried thyme

1 garlic bulb, cloves separated and peeled

Cooking notes:

The za'atar leaves are an added extra here; if you can't source them, leave them out or use thyme instead.

This focaccia will keep for 3–4 days in an airtight container. It can also be frozen and reheated in the oven.

An Instagram fan-turned-friend, Jiji, once invited me to her house in Oman, suggesting that we invite mutual friends over for a potluck. I had planned to make my Mkate wa Ufuta (sesame coconut flatbread, see page 138) – until I rocked up to her kitchen and discovered she had a gas oven. Now, growing up in the UK, it was common to have a gas hob, but a gas oven… I had never even seen one, let alone used one! I couldn't use Jiji's grill, so I had to pivot. The batter is very similar to that of focaccia bread so, in a panic, I threw the dough into a baking dish, sprinkled it with za'atar, dashed over some olive oil and hoped for the best. Forty minutes later, we had our own version of focaccia. Thus, my Za'atar & Garlic Focaccia(ish) was born. I've since retested it, paying attention to the legendary chef Samin Nosrat, who adds a brine to hers. Just please don't tell an Italian that I butchered their focaccia!

Make a salt brine by combining 2 teaspoons of the fine salt with 100ml (scant ½ cup) of boiling water in a bowl. Give it a mix and set aside.

Meanwhile, pour the coconut milk into a bowl. Add the yeast and leave to sit for 5 minutes.

In a large mixing bowl, combine the flour, sugar and remaining fine salt. Stir, then add the egg and pour in the coconut milk and yeast mixture. Beat and combine with your hands for about 8–10 minutes until you have a loose, smooth dough. If you prefer, you can use a stand mixer on high speed for 4 minutes.

Pour in the 125ml (generous ½ cup) of olive oil and mix to combine, then cover the bowl with cling film (plastic wrap) and leave in a warm place for 1½ hours until doubled in size.

Once your dough has risen, wipe a 20 × 33cm (8 × 13in) baking tin or dish with olive oil, then tip the dough into it. Make sure the dough is evenly distributed, then pour your brine evenly over the dough. Sprinkle over the sea salt flakes, za'atar blend and dried za'atar leaves (or thyme), then drizzle over 1 tablespoon of olive oil. Drop the garlic cloves all around the dough, gently pushing them in. Using both hands, stick your fingers into the dough at an angle and gently push all the way down through the dough to create air bubbles. Do not be tempted to pop the bubbles – we need them! Cover the dish and leave to rise for another 45 minutes.

Preheat your oven to 220°C (200°C fan/425°F/Gas 7).

When you're ready to bake, place the focaccia in the oven and reduce the temperature to 200°C/180°C fan/400°F/Gas 6. Bake for 20 minutes, then pour over another 1 tablespoon of olive oil and continue to bake for another 10–20 minutes, depending on how brown you want the top. The bread should be hard on the top, golden and cooked all the way through. Serve and enjoy.

Pistachio & Date Loaf Cake with Whipped Labneh

Serves 6–8

150g (5oz) shelled pistachios, plus extra to decorate
125g (½ cup plus 2 tbsp) caster (superfine) sugar
150g (1 stick plus 2 tbsp) unsalted butter
3 large eggs
210g (scant 1¾ cups) self-raising flour
¼ tsp baking powder
70g (2¼oz) plain yogurt
80ml (generous 5 tbsp) vegetable oil
zest of 1 lemon
1 tsp vanilla extract
150g (5oz) pitted dates, finely chopped

For the whipped labneh topping
250g (9oz) labneh or 300g (10oz) strained Greek yogurt
3 tbsp runny honey, plus extra for drizzling
pinch of sea salt
pomegranate seeds, to decorate (optional)

A simple loaf cake packed with flavours from home, this is one of my go-to sweet recipes for when I'm visiting a friend's house for dinner, or simply want cake to enjoy throughout the week at home. Using whipped labneh instead of a traditional buttercream adds a refreshing, light and slightly sour touch to complement the sweetness of the dates.

Preheat the oven to 200°C (180°C fan/400°F/Gas 6). Grease and double-line a 900g (2lb) loaf tin with baking parchment (parchment paper).

Using a food processor, grind 125g (4½oz) of the pistachios to a fine powder. Roughly chop the rest.

In a large bowl or mixer, mix together the sugar, butter and ground pistachios until you have a creamy pistachio butter. Add the eggs and mix to combine.

Add the flour, baking powder, yogurt, oil, lemon zest and vanilla extract, and fold until everything is combined and you have a smooth batter. Fold in the dates and chopped pistachios.

Pour the batter into the prepared tin and bake for 55–60 minutes, or until a skewer inserted into the middle comes out clean. Check the cake after 35 minutes, and cover the top with foil if it's browning too quickly. Once cooked, leave to cool in the tin for 10 minutes, then transfer to a wire rack to cool completely.

Meanwhile, in a bowl, mix together the labneh or yogurt, honey and a pinch of salt.

Once the loaf is cooled, cut it into thick slices. To serve, top each one with a dollop of the labneh, a drizzle of honey, a sprinkle of sea salt, a few pistachios and some pomegranate seeds, if you like.

The cake (without the labneh topping) will keep for up to a week in an airtight container.

Visheti

Swahili Saffron
Sugared Sable

Makes 40

600g (4⅔ cup) plain (all-purpose)
    flour, plus extra for dusting
150g (1 stick plus 2 tbsp) unsalted
    butter, melted
pinch of salt
vegetable oil, for deep-frying

For the sugar coating
250g (1¼ cups) caster
    (superfine) sugar
1 tsp ground cardamom
good pinch of saffron strands

Cooking notes:

While we fry these, like we do
everything else, you could bake
them if you prefer (though Bibi would
tell you they won't taste the same!).
Be sure to refrigerate before baking,
then bake at 220° C (200° C fan/
425° F/Gas 7) for 10–15 minutes.

Bibi was always known for making some of the best *visheti* in Portsmouth. Every Eid, she would be asked by one of her best friends, Bibi Sharifa, a member of the Zanzibari royal family, to make a big batch for them to enjoy and to share with all the guests who came to visit during the celebrations. I always remember my bibi being overly dramatic about the process and acting like she couldn't do it, but then also basking in all the attention she got when people complimented her on how amazing they were. She would bring out a huge silver pot to make the sugar coating and toss the *visheti* in it; in all honesty, it was a two-man job just to coat them in the sugar. By the time she'd finished the whole batch, we would just be left with a handful to enjoy ourselves, so I always insisted we visit Bibi Sharifa first so I could sit there and eat all the *visheti* we had just sent round. I've called them sables here for context, as they have the same buttery, flaky texture. The only addition is the crystalised spiced sugar coating.

To make the dough, combine the flour, butter and salt in a large bowl and bring together with your hands. As the dough starts to come together, slowly add 100ml (scant ½ cup) of water until everything in the bowl binds together to form a firm dough with no dry bits (depending on your flour, you might not need all the water, so add it a little at a time).

Knead lightly until the dough is smooth and comes together into a ball, then leave to rest for at least 30 minutes.

Once rested, roll out the dough on a lightly floured surface to a thickness of about 2.5cm (1in), then cut it into little diamond shapes around 5cm (2in) long.

Pour the oil into a deep pan to a depth of 10–15cm (4–6in), then place over a high heat. To test if the oil is hot enough for frying, drop one of the diamonds into the oil – if it rises quickly, the oil is hot enough. Add the dough diamonds, working in batches to ensure you don't overcrowd the pan, and fry for 8–10 minutes until golden. Transfer to a plate lined with kitchen paper (paper towels) to drain any excess oil.

To make the crystalised sugar, combine all the ingredients in a large saucepan with 250ml (1 cup plus 1 tablespoon) of water over a high heat. Bring to a boil and boil for 10 minutes, stirring occasionally. We want to bring it close to hard-ball stage.

At this point, remove the pan from the heat and add your fried diamonds. Keep stirring until they are fully coated in the sugar syrup, then spread them out on a baking tray and leave to cool and dry before serving. These will keep in an airtight container for up to 2 weeks.

Dina's Famous Brownies

Serves 12

150g (5oz) dark cooking
    chocolate, roughly chopped
35g (1¼ oz) cocoa powder
170g (1 stick plus 3 tbsp)
    unsalted butter
170g (generous ¾ cup) caster
    (superfine) sugar
55g (generous ¼ cup) soft
    dark brown sugar
3 medium eggs
½ tsp ground cardamom
    or 1 tsp vanilla extract
1 tsp sea salt, plus extra
    for sprinkling
85g (scant ¾ cup) plain
    (all-purpose) flour

I know, who needs another brownie recipe?! But seriously, these are pretty epic. They were my lockdown project, because it was so embarrassing to be cooking online for thousands of people, yet not even be able to make a batch of brownies. So, I spent a good couple of months perfecting (and eating) my recipe, just to achieve the perfect brownie. These have even become TikTok-famous, which means they *must* be fabulous! I simply couldn't resist a sprinkling of cardamom in them (I've officially morphed into my grandmother!) but you can use vanilla if you prefer.

Preheat your oven to 200° C (180° C fan/400° F/Gas 6) and line an 18–20cm (7–8in) square brownie tin with baking parchment (parchment paper), leaving an overhang to help you remove the brownies later.

Begin by placing 110g (3¾oz) of the chocolate in a heatproof bowl with 25g (scant 1oz) of the cocoa powder.

Melt the butter in a saucepan over a high heat until it is vigorously bubbling, then immediately pour it over the chocolate and cocoa in the bowl. Leave to sit for 2 minutes, then whisk until silky smooth. The mixture should have a very loose consistency. Set aside to cool.

In a mixer, combine both sugars with the eggs, cardamom (or vanilla) and salt. Whisk on a medium speed until your batter becomes thick, pale and doubles in size – this will take 3–4 minutes.

Now, still whisking, pour in the melted chocolate mixture. Continue whisking until evenly combined. Sift in your flour and the remaining cocoa powder, then drop in 20g (¾oz) of the remaining chocolate and fold in carefully.

Pour the batter into the prepared tin, then sprinkle over the remaining chopped chocolate. Bake for 10 minutes, then remove from the oven and bang the tin on your work surface three times. Sprinkle the top of the brownie with sea salt, then bake for another 10 minutes. Now stick a skewer into the edge to see if it comes out clean; I usually return it to the oven for another 3 minutes. It seems that 23 minutes is perfect for me, as I get a gooey centre, but you can add an extra 2–3 minutes if you wish, to cook it to your liking.

Remove from the oven and leave to cool in the tin for 10 minutes, then use the baking parchment to lift the brownie out of the tray and leave to cool completely on a wire rack before slicing and serving. This will keep for up to a week in an airtight container.

Saffron Crème Caramel

Serves 8

For the caramel
220g (1 cup plus 2 tbsp)
    granulated or caster
    (superfine) sugar

For the custard
5 eggs
105g (generous ½ cup) caster
    (superfine) sugar
1–2 good pinches of saffron
    strands
250ml (1 cup plus 1 tbsp) double
    (heavy) cream
250ml (1 cup plus 1 tbsp)
    full-fat milk
seeds from ½ vanilla pod or 1 tsp
    vanilla extract (pods are better
    if you can get them)

Growing up, I thought we were the only family who knew about this recipe. My mum used to make it sound so special, as if it was something only she could make. But then again, she made everything sound like that! Our crème caramel flavours would alternate, including cardamom and nutmeg, but saffron was a firm favourite in the family. My mum can practically do this with her eyes closed, but I'd always thought it would be so challenging to make; the eggs and caramel intimidated me, which is probably why I felt my mum was the only one who knew how to make it. But I tested this dish so many times, and ate it at my Auntie Munira's house every day for a week during the Ramadan of 2021, and by the end of that week, I had worked out this silky-smooth recipe, which is honestly so easy to make. Slow and steady wins the race for every element of this dish, especially the caramel – nobody wants to eat burnt sugar!

To make the caramel, place the sugar in a saucepan over a high heat and allow it to gradually melt, gently swirling the pan to help ensure all the sugar melts evenly. The caramel will darken slightly, and you'll know it's ready when it sticks to the back of a spoon and has stringy bits of sugar coming off it. This will take about 2 minutes – once the sugar melts, it's a quick process.

Once you reach this stage, pour the caramel into eight 200ml (scant 1 cup) ramekins and place in the fridge.

To make the custard, begin by whisking your eggs with 50g (¼ cup) of the sugar, then set aside.

Using a pestle and mortar, combine the saffron with 2 teaspoons of the remaining sugar and grind together until the saffron strands have broken down.

In a saucepan, combine the cream, milk, vanilla and remaining sugar, then stir in the saffron sugar and place over a medium heat. You don't want the mixture to boil, but simply to have a slight bubble around the sides; my mum says you should be able to dip your finger into it without the cream burning you.

Pour a tiny amount of the warmed cream into the egg mixture and whisk quickly and constantly to temper the eggs so that they don't scramble.

Recipe continues overleaf

Continue pouring the cream into the egg mixture, adding tiny amounts at a time while whisking. Once it's all incorporated, I keep mixing for a little longer until the cream has cooled down slightly.

Strain the mixture through a sieve to remove any excess froth and foam, then pour it into your ramekins on top of the caramel. Leave to cool.

Preheat the oven to 160° C (140° C fan/325° F/Gas 3), then place the ramekins in the oven for 20–25 minutes – you are looking for a slight jiggle in the middle. Timings can really vary with this dish, so I recommend that you begin to check on the crème caramel after 20 minutes, and monitor every 5 minutes after that if extra time is needed.

Leave to cool completely, then place in the fridge for at least 3–4 hours or overnight before serving.

To serve, you'll need to flip the crème caramel out of the ramekins. I put the ramekins in boiling water to help by slightly melting the sugar at the bottom. Don't be scared to stick a knife in to create an air gap – just be careful not to make lots of dents in the side of the pudding like I do!

Tip:

If you have time, try steeping the saffron in the cream the day before instead of grinding it with the sugar. This will heighten the flavour.

Mango Meringue Tart

Serves 6–8

For the pastry
200g (generous 1½ cups) plain
  (all-purpose) flour, plus extra
  for dusting
½ tsp ground cardamom
100g (scant 1 cup) icing
  (confectioners') sugar
100g (6½ tbsp) unsalted butter,
  cubed
2 large egg yolks
splash of coconut milk , if needed

For the filling
400ml (1¾ cups) mango purée
100ml (scant ½ cup) coconut milk
50g (¼ cup) caster (superfine)
  sugar
2 tsp ground cardamom
zest and juice of 1 lemon
2 large eggs, plus 1 extra yolk

For the meringue
225g (1 cup plus 2 tbsp) caster
  (superfine) sugar
3 large egg whites
1 tsp white vinegar or lemon juice

When I first started my *Dine with Dina* journey, this was my showstopper. I truly thought my creativity had peaked. I was so proud of this tart and would make it continuously, just handing it out to friends, neighbours and family. It was also the first ever social media video I filmed, and I really went for the Nigella vibes, although when I look at it now, it makes me cringe! There are many variations of a mango tart, but this one is special; it was the first recipe that got me excited for my food journey. I added little touches of my heritage for the first time (coconut and cardamom), and people loved it. So I hope you also enjoy its bright and beautiful awesomeness!

Start by making the pastry base. Combine the flour, cardamom, icing sugar and butter in a large bowl and use your hands to rub the butter into the dry ingredients until everything is combined and the mixture resembles breadcrumbs.

Add the egg yolks and continue to massage with your hands until the dough comes together into a ball. You can add a splash of coconut milk if it is slightly dry and needs help coming together.

Transfer the dough to a floured work surface and knead for a couple of minutes until smooth, then wrap in cling film (plastic wrap), flatten into a round and place in the fridge to chill for at least 1–2 hours or overnight.

When you're ready to bake, preheat the oven to 200°C (180°C fan/ 400°F/Gas 6), then remove the cling film and roll out your dough between two pieces of baking parchment (parchment paper) until it's about 1cm (½in) thick. Remove the top piece of baking parchment, then use the other to help you flip the dough into a 20cm (8in) loose-bottomed tart dish. Remove the rest of the baking parchment, making sure the dough is sitting in the dish properly, lining the base and sides. Trim off any excess pastry, then use a fork to prick holes in the base. Cover with baking parchment once more and fill with baking beans or rice.

Bake for 15 minutes, then remove the paper and beans and bake for a further 5 minutes until golden.

Meanwhile, prepare the filling. Combine all the filling ingredients except the eggs in a saucepan over a high heat. Once the mixture begins to bubble around the sides, reduce the heat to medium and simmer for 10–15 minutes until it has reduced by a third and thickened. Remove the pan from the heat.

Recipe continues overleaf

Portsmouth

Whisk the eggs in a bowl, then pour in a small amount of the filling, still whisking continuously, to temper your eggs. Now pour the tempered egg mixture into the pan and continue to whisk, making sure the eggs don't scramble.

Once the base is baked, pour the filling into the tart, then reduce the oven temperature to 180°C (160°C fan/350°F/Gas 4) and bake for 10–15 minutes to set. It should have a slight wobble in the middle; if it's still very loose, leave it for another 5–10 minutes. Leave to cool completely before placing in the fridge to firm up and fully set.

To make the meringue, combine the sugar and 75ml (5 tablespoons) of water in a saucepan over a high heat and bring to the boil, stirring until the sugar has dissolved. If you have a cooking thermometer, it could be useful here; you want the mixture to reach 120°C (248°F).

While the sugar mixture is boiling, begin whisking the egg whites with the vinegar in a mixer at medium speed. Once the mixture has soft peaks, slowly pour in the sugar syrup. Increase the speed of the mixer to high and whisk for a further 6 minutes until stiff peaks form.

You can either pipe the meringue on to the tart, or dollop it on in a more rustic fashion. If you have a blow torch, finish off by torching the meringue. (If you don't have a blow torch, you can pop the tart in a very hot oven for 5 minutes to achieve some colour, then place it in the fridge to chill before serving.) Serve and enjoy the delight of your guests.

Kunafolis

Kunafah Meets Cannoli

~~~~~~~~~~

Makes 10

edible rose petals, to decorate

For the syrup
200g (1 cup) caster
   (superfine) sugar
good pinch of saffron strands
3–4 cardamom pods or 1 tsp
   ground cardamom
juice of ½ lemon

For the shells
500g (1lb 2oz) *kunafah* or
   kataifi pastry
300g (10oz) ghee

For the filling
250g (9oz) mascarpone
400ml (1¾ cups) double
   (heavy) cream
3 tbsp rose water
100g (½ cup) caster
   (superfine) sugar
150g (5oz) shelled pistachios,
   crushed, plus extra to decorate

Cannoli moulds (see Tip)

Tip:

If you don't have cannoli moulds,
making a similar shape out of foil
works just as well.

A "kunafoli" is what happens when a cannoli meets a *kunafah*. It was born from me being greedy and wanting *kunafah* on the go. If you're not familiar with *kunafah*, it's a traditional Middle Eastern dessert filled with cheese or sometimes a thick cream that is encased in a crust made with a shredded filo-type pastry known as *kataifi* (which you can find in Middle Eastern or Mediterranean grocery stores), then soaked in ghee, cooked until golden and crispy and finally drowned in floral and spiced syrups. While the traditional way is always fabulous, this version is something fun to try. It's easy to switch up with flavours through the middle, and great to make for a gathering where everyone can have their own. If you happen to be part Arab and part Italian, this is an ode to you.

Begin by making the syrup. Combine all the syrup ingredients in a medium-sized saucepan with 240ml (1 cup) of water, making sure the water has covered all the sugar.

Place over a high heat. Once the mixture begins to bubble vigorously, start a timer for exactly 10 minutes, then reduce the heat ever so slightly and leave to bubble away, making sure not to stir it.

After 10 minutes, or when your syrup has reached 110°C (230°F), the sugar will have dissolved. Remove from the heat and allow to cool. The syrup will need to be at room temperature before it's poured over your shells. It can be made up to a week in advance and stored in a jar.

To make the shells, preheat the oven to 210°C (190°C fan/410°F/Gas 6½) and line a baking tray with baking parchment (parchment paper).

Unravel the pastry and pull out enough strands so that when they're spread out, it's about 2–3 fingers wide. Take one end of the pastry strands and place in the middle of a cannoli mould. Begin wrapping the pastry around the mould towards one end, making sure you wrap over the start of the pastry so that it doesn't unravel. Once you reach the end, wrap back to the middle and then continue wrapping to the other end. Make sure the pastry strands are spread out rather than bunched together, as this will cause the middle to be too thick. When you reach the other end, wrap slightly towards the middle and finish with the ends of the strands at the bottom of the mould, so that when you place it on a baking tray, the ends will be at the bottom to stop them from opening.

Recipe continues overleaf

241

Repeat with the rest of your pastry and line up the shells on a baking tray.

Heat the ghee in a saucepan over a low heat until liquid. Once it has melted, pour the ghee over all the shells, making sure they are completely soaked. Lift each shell with a pair of tongs to check the bottoms are not dry.

Once you're happy they're fully coated, bake for 20–25 minutes until they are a deep golden brown. As soon as they're cooked, remove from the oven and, using the tongs again, dip them one by one into the syrup, then set aside on a rack to cool while you prepare the filling (place a plate underneath the rack to catch any excess syrup).

For the filling, whisk the mascarpone with an electric hand whisk (hand mixer) in a large bowl to smooth it out to a creamy consistency. Add the rest of the filling ingredients except the pistachios. Whisk the mixture on a high speed until the cream has thickened and formed stiff peaks.

Fold the crushed pistachios into the cream mixture using a spatula, making sure they're evenly distributed.

Once the "kunafoli" shells have cooled, remove the cannoli moulds by gently pushing them out.

To assemble, transfer the cream mixture into a piping bag, with or without a nozzle. Then take one of your "kunafoli" shells and pipe the cream into both ends to make sure it has been filled right through to the middle. Dip each end of the shell into some chopped pistachios to conceal the ends. Repeat with the remaining shells.

Finally, drizzle some syrup over the top and sprinkle over some more chopped pistachios and rose petals. These are best served straight away. The shells will keep for up to a day, but it's best not to fill them until you're almost ready to serve.

Index

Author's Acknowledgments

تَوَكُّل (*tawakkul*) is the Arabic word meaning "to have faith in God's plan" – a word that, having reached the end of *Bahari*, finally makes sense. Sometimes we wish life could have taken a different course. I always wished for that fairy-tale, picket-fence family – a mother, father and all my siblings together. If I had got my wish, I probably wouldn't be writing this. Little did I know that discovering my wholeness and identity wouldn't come from bridging gaps with my father's family, but from connecting to strangers and new friends who could fill in the gaps of my history.

The first and most important acknowledgement is to my mother, Kamlla. Thank you for bringing me into this world and doing everything you could to give me the best start in life, even if that meant sending me to school where I didn't fit in. Most of all, thank you for basically making me your whole world – going above and beyond, playing all the family roles I wished for, staying up until stupid o'clock helping me finish projects I should have completed earlier, and generally doing anything I asked, just so I was never left out. I would travel through every *bahari* to give you anything you want.

To every single person who is reading this book. To the ones who have followed me on social media, shared my work, liked a photo, made a recipe, commented on a video, recommended me for work, come to a supper club, said my name to another person. Honestly, thank you from the bottom of my heart; I would not be in this position without all your support. It has transformed my life and I hope I can continue to bring you content and food that brings you joy.

As the proverb goes, it takes a village to raise a child. *Bahari* and I are proof of that. So many people played a role in supporting my mum to help raise me, and *Bahari* has been raised in the same way. From family members to the new and good friends I met on this journey, so many of whom took me on trips around Oman to learn more about our culture, and gave me recipes, history lessons and most of all, their time: Waheb and Rahma, Maha, Abdullah Al Alawi, Sara, Abdullah Al Shuhi, Zahra and Bibi Mosa, Abdullah Al Lawati, Fatin and Talal, Ali, Kamela, Al Amjaad, Najah and everyone in Oman who has kept our beautiful culture alive.

Moving across the *bahari* to where it all began, thank you to Emma for taking a chance and vibing so well with me; you are the world's best agent. Alex, for testing so many of the recipes to make sure they were perfect. Cara, thank you for seeing the vision I had of *Bahari*, for making sure I had so much freedom with this, for nominating me for the Jane Grigson Award, and most of all, for giving me the BEST team – Lucy, Tania, Tara, Sonali, Kristine, Sam, Georgia and all the people behind the scenes. Thank you to Patsy, who embraced my family with open arms and captured photos in the studio and Oman that spoke to my heart; I hope I can continue to travel the world with you and capture every moment.

To my closest people, thank you for everything you do for me, from putting up with me during this process (and dealing with the amount of stress that came with it!) to helping me at supper clubs, even when I was screaming and shouting; from giving me your pretty kitchens to film in when I needed them, to taking me in when Covid saw me locked down in Oman. Most of all, thank you for simply loving me and being there for me: Kitty, Zahra, Khadija, Farah, Fam, Kammy, Uncle Nas, Auntie Fatma, Sabrina, Dawn, Aqil and Azza, Louise, Hilal and Zahra, Donna and Andy, Clare, Fatamo, Auntie Ray & Rosh.

To Saleh, for being my number-one fan, tirelessly supporting anything I do, and practically moving *jebels* (mountains) to make sure I succeed, I couldn't have done it without you.

A big part of my research and network came from my last job at the Anglo-Omani Society, where I gained so much support from the board, the Omani Embassy in the UK and all the members. It goes without saying that I am beyond grateful to have been in this position and to have been supported so much with my endeavours.

To His Majesty Sultan Haitham bin Tariq Al Said: there is no poise and kindness better suited than yours to lead Oman. Thank you for everything you continue to do for us.

To Bibi, a big part of *Bahari*. Thank you for being unapologetically you. The most incredible, challenging grandmother who speaks her mind, loves herself the most, but loves to cook for her family more. You've provided countless joy for me and the thousands who have enjoyed watching you on Instagram. And to Gigi, for being Bibi's big brother, a father figure to me, for always being my cheerleader and for sharing countless stories of Zanzibar with me. I love you both. Thank you for sharing your past and your present.

To the ones not with us: Babu, Uncle Abbas and my father, Mahmood. And on that last note, while my mother never got to live out her fairy-tale dreams in Oman with her greatest love, my father, she instilled all of that passion into me. I've always felt like the glue that holds her close to Oman and him. While he is no longer with us, I cook for her, him and all the Omani people, wherever the *bahari* has taken them.

About the Author

Dina Macki is a British-Omani food writer, presenter and recipe developer. Her work has a strong focus on Omani and Zanzibari culture and the food influenced by those countries as well as the wider Middle East, East Africa and her upbringing in the UK. Dina has been determined to shift the narrative on what Middle Eastern food is and try to better educate and introduce people to the diverse and varied cuisines that span the 21 countries. She is a massive food anthropology nerd and loves to get lost in learning the origins and history behind what we eat. Day to day, Dina's work spans writing recipes and developing dishes in the UK and internationally, consulting for restaurants and hotels in the Middle East, as well as sharing her passion through content creation. Whatever she is working on, she bridges the West and the East to bring delicious, innovative recipes that pay homage to her heritage.

Publisher's acknowledgments

DK would like to thank Clare Skeats for design development work, Dr Ida Hadjivayanis for providing a sensitivity read, Kathryn Glendenning for proofreading, and Ruth Ellis for providing the index. The publisher would also like to thank Georgia Quinn and Sam Reeves for photography assistance, and Kristine Jakobsson for assistance with food styling.

Picture Credits

All photography by Patricia Niven except images on pages: 10ca, 10c, 10clb, 10cb, 10b, 10br, 94bl, 94br, 166, 167, 175, 176, 177, 205, 206, 207, 214 by Dina Macki and family; and 94t by Adnan Daheesh.

(Key: a-above; b-below/bottom; c-centre; f-far; l-left; r-right; t-top).

DK LONDON
Editorial Manager Cara Armstrong
Project Editor Lucy Sienkowska
Senior Designer and Jacket Designer Tania Gomes
Senior Production Editor Tony Phipps
Senior Production Controller Stephanie McConnell
Jacket and Sales Material Coordinator Emily Cannings
Art Director Maxine Pedliham
Publishing Director Katie Cowan

Editorial Tara O'Sullivan
Illustration and Jacket Artwork Tom Abbiss Smith
Photography Patricia Niven
Food Styling Sonali Shah
Prop Styling Rachel Vere

DK DELHI
Managing Art Editor Neha Ahuja Chowdhry
DTP Designers Satish Chandra Gaur, Raman Panwar
DTP Coordinator Pushpak Tyagi
Pre-production Manager Balwant Singh
Creative Head Malavika Talukder

First American Edition, 2024
Published in the United States by DK Publishing
1745 Broadway, 20th Floor, New York, NY 10019

Text copyright © Dina Macki 2024
Dina Macki has asserted her right to be identified
as the author of this work.
Artwork copyright © Tom Abbiss Smith, 2024
Photography copyright © Patricia Niven, 2024
Copyright © 2024 Dorling Kindersley Limited
DK, a Division of Penguin Random House LLC
24 25 26 27 28 10 9 8 7 6 5 4 3 2 1
001–336611–Feb/2024

A catalog record for this book
is available from the Library of Congress.
ISBN: 978-0-7440-9235-6

DK books are available at special discounts when purchased in bulk for sales promotions, premiums, fund-raising, or educational use. For details, contact: DK Publishing Special Markets, 1745 Broadway, 20th Floor, New York, NY 10019
SpecialSales@dk.com

Printed and bound in China

www.dk.com

MIX
Paper | Supporting responsible forestry
FSC™ C018179

This book was made with Forest Stewardship Council™ certified paper - one small step in DK's commitment to a sustainable future.
For more information go to www.dk.com/our-green-pledge

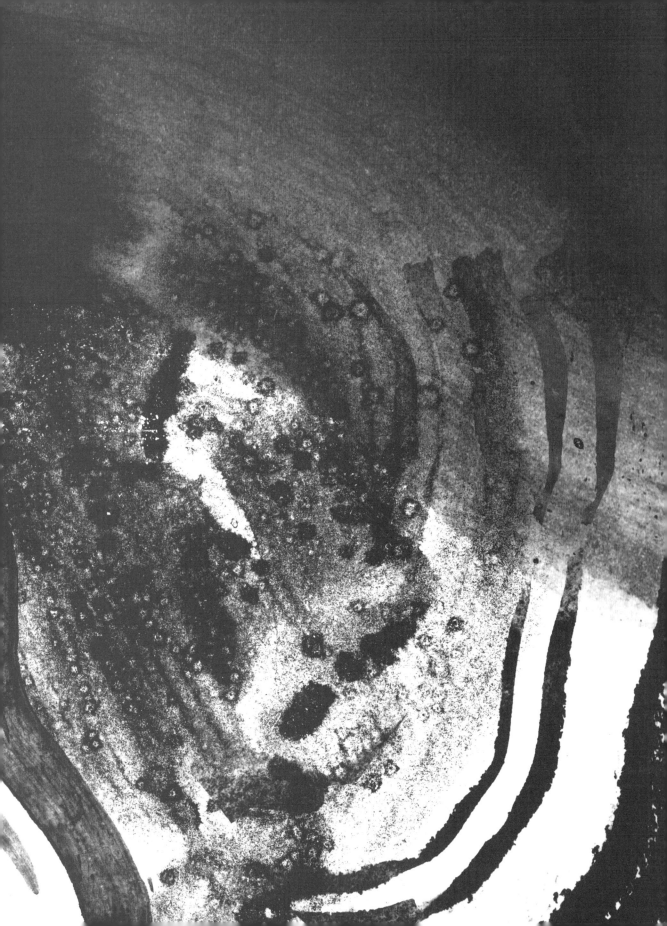